"Everyone, it seems, claims to like the new front yard,
yet everyone expects others not to like it." – Stan Cox

Edible Estate #1 Salina, Kansas

"We're a pretty average family, in a pretty average neighborhood.
If we can make it work, anybody can." – Michael Foti

Edible Estate #2 Lakewood, California

"When we watch our son nibble leaf after leaf of cinnamon basil, toss a salad for our
parents from just-picked lettuces and herbs, . . . and brew a pot of fresh mint tea to share
with friends, . . . the work before us doesn't seem so daunting." – Michelle Christman

Edible Estate #3 Maplewood, New Jersey

"[The residents] use the garden as a starting point for a wider discussion on their
neighborhood and the improvements they want to see." – Carole Wright

Edible Estate #4 London, England

"When I start supper and I notice I don't have a certain herb, I just look out my kitchen
window to see what is out there and then go pick whatever I need." – Maricela Rodriguez

Edible Estate #5 Austin, Texas

"I have noticed that traffic slows down in front of my house, like I have my own personal
speed bump. Neighbors I had only waved to from a distance as they passed in their cars now
stop or approach me on the street to talk." – Clarence Ridgley

Edible Estate #6 Baltimore, Maryland

"Within a short time students began encouraging their families to start their
own gardens at home." – Susan Fuelling, Laurie Hopkins, and Dale Freyberger

Edible Estate #7 Descanso Demonstration Garden, La Cañada Flintridge, California

"It is easy to forget that under the asphalt of Tenth Avenue there is soil . . . [and] if that
soil was released from its stony tomb, it could grow food again." – Eric W. Sanderson

Edible Estate #8 Lenape Edible Estate: Manhattan, New York, New York

Whenever there are in any country uncultivated lands and unemployed poor, it is clear that the laws of property have been so far extended as to violate natural right. The earth i given as a common stock for man to labor and live on. The small landowners are the most precious part of a state. – **Thomas Jefferson**

EDIBLE ESTATES

ATTACK ON THE FRONT LAWN

A Project by Fritz Haeg

with texts by

Will Allen

Diana Balmori

Rosalind Creasy

Fritz Haeg

Michael Pollan

Eric W. Sanderson

Lesley Stern

2ND EDITION

METROPOLIS BOOKS

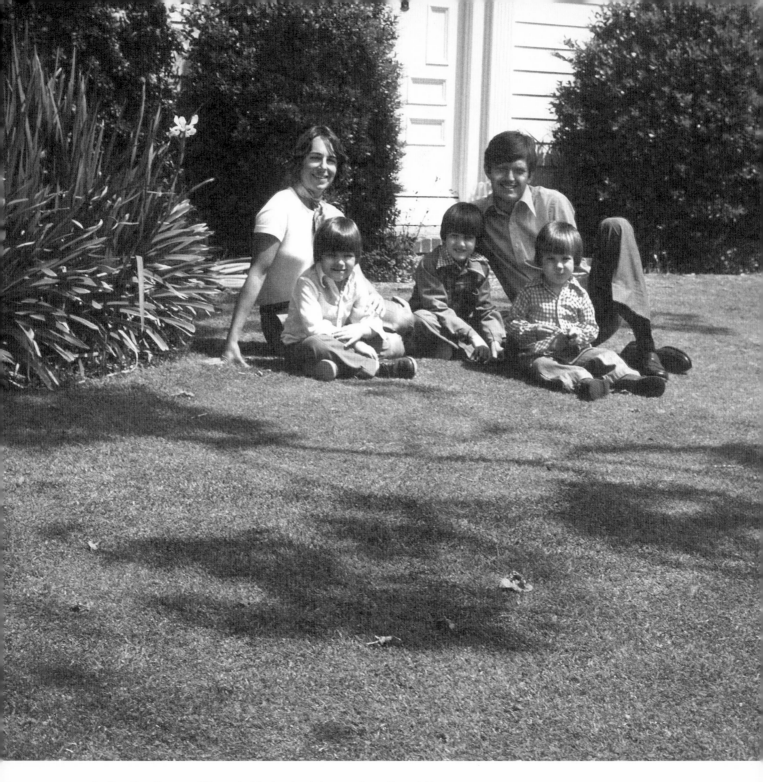

For Mary O. and Lawrence P. Haeg, who introduced me to lawn mowing and bean picking

CONTENTS

PREFACE

This book is a collection of illustrated stories of people's experiences publicly growing food where they live. It documents the eight Edible Estates regional prototype gardens that I have planted since 2005 and, in most cases, it includes personal accounts from the gardeners themselves. Be advised that this is not a glossy volume of perfectly manicured aspirational gardens that you envy but can never hope to achieve yourself; nor is it a comprehensive how-to guide to growing your own food—there are plenty of resources of this type, including *Edible Landscaping* by Rosalind Creasy, a contributor to this book. The garden stories presented here, with all of their challenges and rewards, are intended to reveal something about how we are living today and to offer you some inspiration to plant your own version of an Edible Estate.

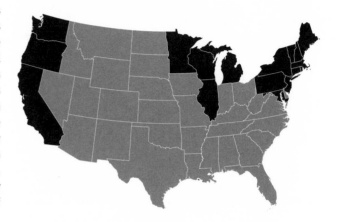

By attacking the front lawn, an essential icon of the American Dream, my hope is to ignite a chain reaction of thoughts that question other antiquated conventions of home, street, neighborhood, city, and global networks that we take for granted. If we see that our neighbor's typical lawn instead can be a beautiful food garden, perhaps we begin to look at the city around us with new eyes. The seemingly inevitable urban structures start to unravel as we recognize that we have a choice about how we want to live and what we want to do with the places we have inherited from previous generations. No matter what has been handed to us, each of us should be given license to be an active part in the creation of the cities that we share, and in the process, our private land can be a public model for the world in which we would like to live.

The Edible Estates project is about people and their relationships to each other and to their environment. It did not originate from thoughts about lawns or food or gardens; these are vehicles with which to engage larger issues of the human condition today. At the end of 2004 we watched as the media informed us that the United States had just split into red and blue. I was devastated by the results of the election, but I was also alarmed by the popular story that our country was cleft in two, with supposedly irreconcilable, opposing points of view. For us or against us: it seemed like the lines had been drawn and you were meant to take a side.

I was born in Minnesota, schooled in Pennsylvania and Italy, worked in Connecticut, later settled in New York, and now live in California. In spite of my migrations I realized how limited my experience of my own country was. I was also beginning to feel uneasy with the insular, self-referential, and hermetic nature of the contemporary art and architecture community, of which I consider myself a part. Are we elitist, separatist, or just disinterested? Today's media climate allows you to filter your news and stories to only those with which you agree. Have we given up on any sort of real dialogue and returned to our corners to talk among ourselves? What is the appropriate response to the current state of the world, its politics, climate, and economics? What should I do next? How I could *not* make work about these things? They took on an urgency that I had not felt before.

After the elections I left for a six-week residency in Australia. I wanted to use this break as an opportunity to consider the direction of my work. I spent time first at the Royal Botanic Gardens in Sydney and then at the Daintree Rainforest and the Great Barrier Reef. The astounding diversity and extreme vitality of these environments had a profound impact on me, as

I realized how completely dependent each organism is upon the others. Remove one and the whole system can eventually degrade and collapse. This seemed to be a good lesson at a time when our obsession with independence is perhaps naive and oversimplified. Sharing resources—water, air, streets, neighborhoods, cities, countries, and a planet—all of our destinies are more intertwined than ever.

Upon my return I had no idea what direction my work should take, apart from some vague desire to do something in the geographic center of the United States, which would be Kansas. I envisioned some sort of symbolic act to engage with the entirety of the country, not just the narrow cultural circles on the coasts. I wanted to reclaim a sense of citizenship in this country, which seemed headed away from everything I believed in. My mind went to the westward movement of the pioneers across that state and the modest sod houses they constructed for themselves. Did they know where they were headed?

That winter curator Stacy Switzer invited me to give a lecture at Grand Arts, a project space in Kansas City, Missouri. Upon hearing my ideas for Kansas, Stacy invited me to produce something in Salina, which happens to be nearly the exact geographic center of the United States. My focus quickly went to that iconic American space, the front lawn, and all the wasted potential it represents. Grafting domestic agriculture onto this space seemed ripe with possibilities. Here was a place to really engage all Americans, slicing through economic and social strata, geographic regions, and political affiliations. With Stacy's support the first Edible Estate garden was generously commissioned by the Salina Art Center and planted, symbolically, on Independence Day of 2005. The stories of that garden and the others that followed are told in the second edition of this book, which includes eight regional prototype gardens.

In the eighteen months since *Edible Estates: Attack on the Front Lawn* was first published, the global economy went into a tailspin, businesses failed, employment plummeted, and food prices soared, but sales of vegetable seeds and the number of first-time home vegetable gardeners went way up. With the collapse of the housing market, our relationship to the place where we live has also changed radically. The view of the home as a piggy bank of ever increasing wealth to be constantly leveraged by selling up the market, lamented by Edible Estate #1 owner Stan Cox (see p. 64) abruptly ended. As people stay put, a new sense of stability develops, and of course a garden is something that you plant only if you intend to stay where you are for a while. The luxurious, generic green lawn is the first step in marketing a house for sale, and who in his or her right mind would replace it with an eccentric, unique vegetable garden when looking for a quick flip and profit?

Perhaps the most exciting and visible development since the publication of the first edition has been the planting of a modest vegetable garden by First Lady Michelle Obama. With the origins of the Edible Estates project firmly rooted in presidential politics, it is gratifying to be able to bookend the 2004 re-election of George W. Bush with the election of Barack Obama and the subsequent planting of the organic vegetable garden on the South Lawn of the White House. Something that may have seemed unthinkable a year and a half ago now seems like an inevitable next step for a society that has become increasingly interested in its food and where it comes from.

Soon after the White House vegetable garden was planted, the *Guardian* invited me to share my thoughts on it; that text is reprinted on the following pages.

Why the White House Garden Matters

Has one vegetable garden ever generated so much excitement or debate? A few details about the new White House vegetable garden caught my attention.

It is 1,100 square feet. This is a garden sized for a family. In my experience removing front lawns and planting Edible Estates prototype gardens across the United States, the Obama garden is about the size of the average American front lawn. Most Americans should be able to imagine themselves planting something about this size in front of their houses over a weekend with the help of some friends and neighbors. Of course, I would have preferred that the Obamas remove the entire South Lawn of the White House. I imagine a combination of fruit tree orchards, wild berry patches, and edible-flower and grass meadows. But since this new First Family garden should be a model to inspire every American family, perhaps a modest 1,100 square feet is the best way to start the revolution.

There will be tomatillos and cilantro but no beets. The Obamas love Mexican food, and Barack does not like beets. This is a garden planted for the personal tastes of the family that will be eating from it. It is not just a pretty garden or an empty symbol, but a place for a family to grow the food that they like to eat on the land that is around them. They have selected fifty-five varieties of vegetables and herbs according to their tastes, and every American family can inspect that list and imagine what it would plant instead. Where are the tomatoes? Why so much spinach? Can I grow blueberries where I live? The uniform lawns surrounding our homes all deny our diverse climates and cultures. Neighborhood streets lined with edible gardens like the Obamas' would all be different, celebrating our individual tastes.

It will be visible from E Street. Will tourists linger at the South Lawn fence hoping to catch a glimpse of Malia and Sasha weeding? We will all be able to watch the garden grow through the seasons and evolve over the years. This is a vegetable and herb garden in front of the house, and it is meant to be seen. Since the late 1940s the sterile industrial landscape of the lawn has come

to dominate our streets. This divisive and repressive aesthetic has been sold to us as the only acceptable surface to present to our neighbors. But our ideas of beauty are always shifting, and soon the front lawn will be considered an ugly vestige of an ignorant time. Why did they water, weed, mow, fertilize, and pollute for a ceremonial space they never even used? With the Obamas giving us an organic vegetable garden to look at, we are taking steps toward a more thoughtful, beautiful, healthy, and productive landscape.

Fifth graders from Bancroft Elementary School helped plant it. Many American children today do not see evidence that food comes out of the ground or experience the pleasure of eating food fresh from plants. Instead, their diets are causing epidemic childhood illnesses. The introduction of a food-producing garden into their early lives is our best hope for changing the situation in a meaningful way. In my on-the-street garden-planting experiences from Austin to London, it is always the children who are the first ones on the scene and the most excited to help. They tend to be the least skeptical and the most hopeful about the future prospects for the garden. We should have a garden like the Obamas' wherever there are children.

A beekeeper will tend two hives for honey, and ladybugs and praying mantises will help control harmful bugs. Fully sanctioned and welcomed critters at the White House! This is perhaps more exciting than the garden itself. We know that the lawn is essentially ecological genocide; everything but the precious blades of grass must die in the name of that luxurious green carpet. Pesticides indiscriminately decimate the bugs that are pests and any other forms of life that get in the way. An organic garden is not an island, even if it is surrounded by a lawn.

It is encouraging to see this acknowledged with the welcoming of the partner animals that will make pollination, pest control, and the production of food possible without chemicals.

Planting beds will be fertilized with White House compost and crab meal from the Chesapeake Bay. I love local details—they make gardens special and lawns boring. So the thought of crab meal from the local bay coming to the South Lawn is a thrilling development. The rest of us can read about that and ask what local resources could feed our gardens. Seaweed from the coast? Manure from the farm? And what about the First Family's compost pile? We need to see images of that and find out where it will be located. I would advocate for a very visible and privileged location, perhaps at the ceremonial south entrance to the White House, where Barack can show off the rich pile of decomposing banana peels and coffee grinds to visiting heads of state. As any gardener knows, the compost pile is the engine of the garden, the place where yesterday's "waste" becomes tomorrow's fertility. What better message could there be for us today?

The total cost is $200. They could have planted a very elaborate and expensive garden that might have been more worthy of its privileged location in front of the White House, but I am so pleased that they planted something modest and cheap. Sales of vegetable plants and seeds are soaring along with the cost of food. Americans are rediscovering the economic benefits and perhaps even the daily pleasure of being outside and growing food where they live. Of course, there are probably some buried expenses not included in the $200 price tag, and some people will argue that you need to spend a small fortune and most of your time on such a garden. But an important message has been sent: Here is something anyone should be able to afford to do at home.

Is this too much hyperbole for one little garden? Am I placing too much significance on such a simple act? In the face of trillion-dollar deficits and billion-dollar bailouts, perhaps it is exactly the modesty of the gesture that makes this message so welcome right now.

Fritz Haeg, editorial, Guardian, *March 25, 2009*

I would like to recognize the heroes and friends who have in some way been responsible for the development of Edible Estates. Agnes Denes made a wheat field in lower Manhattan that I still remember reading about in *Time* magazine at the age of thirteen. Meg Webster made gardens and streams at museums that were a revelation to me in my teens and had a profound influence on the direction of my work. Laurie Palmer, a visiting art professor at Carnegie Mellon University, introduced me to the possibility for ecological thought to invade art practice. Gordon Matta-Clark is the artist I can't stop thinking about. His short span of work—which included removing walls, planting subterranean trees, making architecture out of dumpsters, buying up "fake estates," and making food for friends as a ceremony—is more relevant than ever. Nils Norman is a thoughtful artist and supportive peer whose work is an inspiration. Mel Chin's gardens, including his *Revival Field* in St. Paul, Minnesota, have been important precedents. Katie Holten makes fake trees, plants weeds, and generally feels like a comrade. Ant Farm's inflatables, actions, buildings, drawings, public performances, and American renegade spirit have always captivated my imagination. Buckminster Fuller was thinking globally in a way that few had before him. He was interested in effecting meaningful global change with precise, modest acts that we are in need of again today.

Although I have listed the credits for each of the gardens later in these pages, I would especially like to thank those who have played a critical role in the realization of the Edible Estates gardens to date. Mark Allen at Machine Project, Dan Danzig at Millard Sheets Gallery, and curator Irene Tsatsos made the Lakewood garden and exhibitions possible. Sara Grady was a devoted partner and Gardener's Supply a generous sponsor for the garden in Maplewood. The Durfee Foundation displayed its confidence in the project with grants supporting the Lakewood and London gardens. Stuart Comer of the Tate Modern and curators November Paynter and Kathy Noble helped realize the London garden and later exhibition through kind hospitality and tireless support. Brian Sullivan and David Brown extended the invitation to create a project for Descanso Gardens; Elizabeth Dunbar at Arthouse created the opportunity for the Austin garden and related community workshops to happen in the context of my exhibition there; and Irene Hofmann at the Contemporary Museum served as a combination curator, fund-raiser, gardener, and hostess in Baltimore. Finally, the Lenape

garden was made possible with sponsorship from Gardenburger LLC and the collective efforts of Amy Gavaris and Drew Becher at New York Restoration Project; Danya Sherman, Robert Hammond, and Peter Mullan at Friends of the High Line; Kris Slava at Ovation; Bettina Korek at ForYourArt; and the brilliant inspiration of Eric W. Sanderson and his Mannahatta Project.

The work on both editions of this book coincided with residencies in the New Hampshire woods of the MacDowell Colony, where I had the privilege to slow down, focus my thoughts, and reflect on the project as a whole. I would like to thank Matthew Au, Katie Bachler, Aubrey White, and Claire Zitzow for their hours of researching and assisting on the project. This book benefited from the keen eye of copy editor Meghan Conaton and the vision of graphic designers Kimberly Varella at Department of Graphic Sciences and Stacy Wakefield. Finally, I thank one of the earliest supporters of the project, the editor and publisher responsible for these pages, Diana Murphy at Metropolis Books. With each new book she produces, another facet of her unfolding vision is revealed, demonstrating how thoughtful and beautiful design can offer us rich possibilities for better living and catalyze provocative social and environmental change.

Since this book was first published, in 2008, I have traveled widely across the United States and Europe on invitations to talk about these garden experiences with everyone from urban engineers in London and architects in Anchorage to gardeners in Madison and college art students in Gainesville. Bridging audiences of activists, architects, artists, environmentalists, foodies, gardeners, homeowners, landscape designers, and urban planners is gratifying but can also be a challenge, since it is impossible to fully satisfy all of them with one book. Though each may be approaching the topics with a specific agenda, they all share a delight in gardens and an interest in examining alternatives to the direction in which we are headed as a society. It is with this spirit of a collective and common desire to explore other ways of living that I hope you will approach this book. It will inevitably not contain everything you are looking for, and perhaps it will leave you wanting more, but it also might invite you to take a second look out your front door, which is a start.

Fritz Haeg
Los Angeles, California, October 2009

BEAUTY AND THE LAWN: A BREAK WITH TRADITION

Diana Balmori

The lawn has been attacked by me and by many others as an environmental hazard. *Redesigning the American Lawn*, which I wrote with Herbert Bormann and Gordon Geballe (1993), was followed by a torrent of books and articles reassessing the lawn. That reassessment was needed. The lawn had become an invisible industry that created serious environmental effects. Our attack on the lawn allowed us to cast a fresh look at something we took for granted. We used ecological values to challenge traditional aesthetic values, and a socially treasured object became suspect. In the end, nothing less than the abandonment of this developed and admired form is required.

The smooth manicured lawn demands a monoculture of one or two species of grasses; every other plant must be carefully removed or exterminated. Achieving the perfect greenness requires the addition of nitrogen and phosphorus. These chemicals enter groundwater and drainage systems, which eventually empty into streams and rivers, spurring algae growth that consumes the oxygen in the water, killing all other forms of life. Floating dead fish are one of the visible signs that water has been polluted.

The elimination of all other species of interloping plants is also achieved through the application of chemicals, with the resulting pollution of air and groundwater, and direct human exposure through skin contact with the grass. In the nineteenth century, clover was commonly planted with grass; it provides nitrogen for the lawn without contaminating the water supply. But clover subsequently came to be seen as an imperfection, something to be eradicated from lawns. Making a perfect green carpet also requires a great deal of water, a poor use of our dwindling water supplies. The manicured image is dependent, too, on gasoline-run machinery, equipment that is much less efficient and more polluting than an automobile.

The case has been scientifically made. But the American lawn is a carefully tended object that society as a whole has embraced as an icon of beauty. Its beauty was put to good use in the nineteenth century: by Frederick Law Olmsted, to create romantic and beautiful swards in the many parks he designed (30 percent of Central Park is still covered by lawn); and by the planners of the newly developed suburbs, in which a fenceless continuous front lawn would produce an environment that gave the illusion of a park with houses in it.

I am interested in moments when we transgress, when we cross the line to take down such a powerful symbol as the lawn, whose beauty has given us enormous satisfaction. Today we are in a critical phase, as one of our concepts of beautiful open space is being transformed through cultural change. Our ecological knowledge demands that we give up our lawns. This icon is no longer viable, not in the same form.

The meadow of mixed grasses and flowers is one of many possible successors to the lawn. Behind it are echoes of the prairie, a landscape that at one time covered a third of the United States but today remains only in isolated pockets in different states. The meadow has romantic connotations of an American past, and evokes the nostalgia that later generations who did not live in them attach to bygone places.

The prairie was a spontaneous landscape. It belonged to its locale; hosted multiple species, thus fostering biotic diversity; and did not require water or additional chemicals. A nascent industry will soon offer many varieties of the prairie. Then today's Capability Browns, Humphry Reptons, and Olmsteds will get to work and may convert American front or backyards and parks into new icons of beauty.

Another alternative to the lawn is a productive garden such as one of Fritz Haeg's Edible Estates. After three generations have distanced themselves from farming and farms have become industrial giants cultivating thousands of acres, a new interest in where our food comes from has fostered gardens and small farms that supply food for college kitchens and farmers' markets. People are devoting parts of their lawns to orchards or vegetable gardens, rediscovering the seasons and which delicacies each one yields.

Beauty has many dimensions, and they are not only aesthetic. Beauty is a rather more complex concept that has cultural and moral dimensions. Will you look at this established icon deemed beautiful for generations with the same eyes once you know the effects it has on our environment? Ecological thinking has transformed how we see the lawn, and our concept of beauty has been transformed with it.

STORIES FROM THE FRONT YARD

FULL-FRONTAL GARDENING

Fritz Haeg

The front lawn is so deeply embedded in our national psyche that we don't really see it any more, at least for what it actually is. What is that chasm between house and street? Why is it there? Or rather, why is nothing there?

I grew up surrounded by a lawn. This is a common American phenomenon. Perhaps the first growing thing most of us experience as a child is, indeed, a mowed grassy surface. How are a child's ideas of "the natural" affected by this? Of course, there is nothing remotely natural about a lawn. It is an industrial landscape disguised as organic plant material.

As a teenager I passed many weekend afternoons mowing the lawn and I loved it. The more overgrown the lawn, the greater the sense of satisfaction as you roar over it to reveal that crisp trimmed surface and fresh grassy smell. I suppose most of my outdoor time as a youth was spent on a lawn. It is the first

defensive ring between the family unit and everything beyond. It is the border control that physically and psychologically keeps wilderness, city, and strangers at a safe distance.

THE ENGLISH ESTATE
The lawn has its roots in England and is the foundation for any proper English landscape. In spite of the unnatural repression of all other plants, a lawn of mowed grass makes some sense in England, with its regular rainfall and cool climate. Animals grazed, lawn games were played, and the wilderness had been civilized and kept at bay with the crisp line where the grass ended.

The front lawn was born of vanity and decadence, under the assumption that fertile land was infinite. The English estate owner in Tudor times would demonstrate his vast wealth by *not* growing food on the highly visible fecund property in front of his residence. Instead this vast swath of land would become a stage of ornamental green upon which he could present his immense pile of a house. Look how rich I am! Similarly, the plumage of the male peacock advertises well-being and virility, and when he fans his feathers, he shows he can spare the enormous energy necessary to put on such a phenomenal display. The

Once that fertile farmland in front of the English estate had been turned into a sterile monoculture, where did the cultivation of food happen? Out of view, of course, hidden in a remote section of the property where visitors and the lord of the estate would never see it. This was perhaps the beginning of the notion that plants that produce food are ugly and should not be seen. Today the idea has played itself out at an industrial global scale, with our produce grown on the other side of the planet. The only landscape worthy of the public eye is made of ornamentals, trimmed within an inch of their lives, inhospitable to other creatures, always the same and never changing with the seasons.

better the display, the healthier the peacock, and the more likely he is to attract a mate. In the case of the English estate owner, the expanse of green signals financial health and power. This obsession with the lawn is, I believe, almost entirely a male phenomenon. It is an enticing and toxic brew of male seduction, aggression, and domination. Whether intended to attract a mate, demonstrate wealth, impress his friends, or control every bit of nature that surrounds him, the lawn is covered with the fingerprints of masculine tendencies.

THE BIRTH OF THE AMERICAN DREAM

Even if you have never seen Thomas Jefferson's Monticello, in the hills of Virginia, you know it well. It is still the de facto prototype for the American home. You may recognize its prominent features in many contemporary housing developments: the Palladian windows, the white-columned portico, the red brick facade, and the vast green lawn that dominates the landscape around it. Jefferson's house is very much in the tradition of the English estate. Master of all it surveys, wilderness at bay, anchored on the lawn, the illusion of absolute independence—this is still the model for most Americans' real-estate fantasies.

Jefferson had a well-documented love affair with his kitchen garden, which was really more like a small domestic farm. He kept a detailed diary of its growth and evolution through the seasons and years. He lavished upon it devoted attention and care. It seems to have been one of the great passions of his life. And yet, where did he locate it? The house is clearly the focus of the site, on top of the hill and the center of all power. But his beloved garden is hidden from view, to the side and slightly down the hill. The lawn and flowerbeds are laid out in soft decorative curves, a pleasing complement to the house and obviously meant for pleasure. The hidden productive garden, however, is terraced on a long straight bed, divided into a grid, crops arrayed neatly in rows. With that binary division between sterile ornamental pleasure and pragmatic secluded production,

Jefferson reinforced an attitude toward our national landscape that we are still living with today. Roll out the lawn and hide the crops! Given Monticello's early influence, how would American neighborhoods look today if Jefferson had decided to plant his food in front of his house instead?

The world wars left many farms across the United States short-handed. The federal government embarked on a campaign to encourage Americans to do their part by growing food on their own property. First called war gardens and later victory gardens, they quickly became popular across the country. By the end of World War II, over 80 percent of American households were growing some of their own food. Within months after Victory Day this activity quickly subsided. With its demise went the widespread knowledge among most Americans of how to grow their own food.

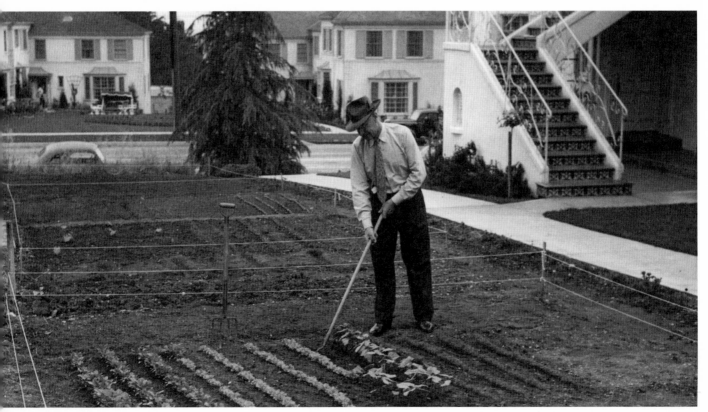

Fritz Haeg Full-Frontal Gardening

In *Schrebergärten* in Germany today we see some evidence of what a neighborhood of victory gardens might have looked like. These community gardens were first developed as a social program in nineteenth-century Berlin. Residents were allotted plots in green belts at the periphery of the city, giving them the opportunity to seek respite from the confines of their urban lives by traveling a short distance to work in a food and flower garden. On each plot they would construct a small cottage, and many relocated to these tiny shelters after the city was bombed during World War II. Visiting these gardens, which can still be found throughout Germany, is like stepping into either some agrarian past or a utopian future. Each yard is a diverse and abundant display of food growing. Most of the gardens are meticulously groomed and maintained to such an extent that it becomes clear this is not just about sustenance; they are also meant to be delightful pleasure gardens. In this otherworldly neighborhood of gardens, modest human quarters are subservient to the land that feeds the residents.

Back in the United States, the introduction of the leisure weekend, the abundance of fresh water, the production of industrial pesticides, the availability of the lawn mower and cheap gas, and the rise of home ownership with the explosion of new suburban housing developments in the 1940s and '50s all set the stage for the unfurling of the great American lawn as we know it today. Its puritanical aspects seem suited to the Eisenhower years of good manners. Is there a connection between landscape and hairstyles? Trimmed grass and crew cuts seem like obvious companions. Nature is not something you surrender to; rather, if you use enough industrial force, you can bend it to your will. This premise and the assumption that land and natural resources were in infinite supply are in part what gave us today's lawned landscape.

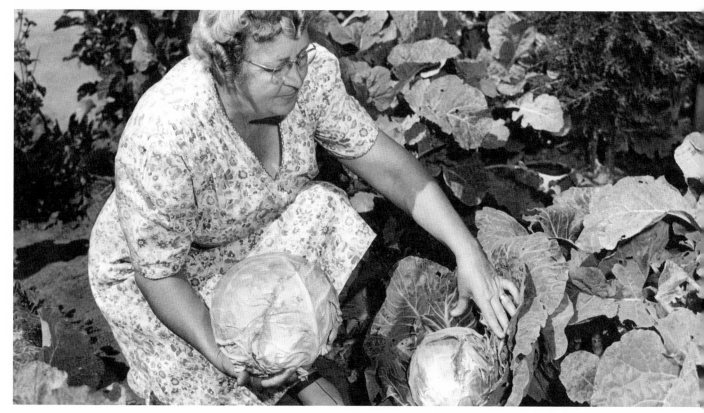

HINDSIGHT AND FORESIGHT

It's easy to be the Monday morning quarterback when we evaluate what previous generations have handed down to us. Coming out of a depression and two world wars, our elders had every right to celebrate the comforts and conveniences of industrial progress. Its hidden long-term costs and a blind faith in its capacity to solve any problem created a sense that things could only get better. This is an optimism we have lost for the moment, as we are coming to terms with the limits of our resources and land.

Now that we know more about what constitutes a healthy life for future generations, it's time for some questions. Before we spread out farther, how do we want to occupy the space we have already claimed? Why do we dedicate so much property to a space that has so minor a function and requires many precious resources and endless hours to maintain, while contaminating our air and water? The American front lawn is now almost entirely symbolic. Aristocratic English spectacle and drama have degenerated into a bland garnish for our endless suburban sprawl and alienation. The monoculture of one plant species covering our neighborhoods from coast to coast celebrates puritanical homogeneity and mindless conformity.

An occasional lawn for recreation can be a delight, but most of them are occupied only when they are being tended. Today's lawn has become the default surface for any defensible private space. If you don't know what to put there, plant grass seed and keep watering. Driving around most neighborhoods you will see lush beds of grass being tended on narrow unused strips of land. In the United States we plant more grass than any other crop: currently lawns cover more than thirty million acres. Given the way we lavish precious resources on it and put it everywhere that humans go, aliens landing in any American city today would assume that grass must be the most precious earthly substance of all.

Yet the lawn devours resources while it pollutes. It is maniacally groomed with mowers and trimmers powered by the two-stroke motors that are responsible for much of our greenhouse gas emissions. Hydrocarbons from mowers react with nitrogen oxides in the presence of sunlight to produce ozone. To eradicate invading plants the lawn is drugged with pesticides and herbicides, which are then washed into our water supply with sprinklers and hoses, dumping our increasingly rare fresh drinking resource down the gutter.

Meanwhile, at the grocery store we confront our food. Engineered fruits and vegetables wrapped in plastic and Styrofoam are cultivated not for taste but for appearance, uniformity, and ease of transport, then sprayed with chemicals to inhibit the diseases and pests that thrive in an unbalanced ecosystem.

The produce in the average American dinner is trucked 1,500 miles to reach our plates. We don't know where our fruits and vegetables came from or who grew them. Perhaps we have even forgotten that plants were responsible for the mass-produced meal we are consuming. This detachment from the source of our food breeds a careless attitude toward our role as custodians of the land that feeds us. Perhaps we would reconsider what we put down the drain, on the ground, and in the air if there was more direct evidence that we will ultimately ingest it.

The garden began behind walls, a truce, a compromise, between human need and natural resource. In most languages the word "garden" derives from the root "enclosure." The garden walls protected human cultivation from the wild threats in the untamed expanses. Now that a wilderness unaffected by human intervention no longer exists, the garden walls have fallen. The enclosed, cultivated space protected behind the house is no longer a worthwhile model. The entire street must be viewed as a garden, and by extension the entire city we are tending, and beyond. We have intervened on all levels of environmental function, and with no walls remaining we have taken on the role of planetary gardener by default.

EDIBLE ESTATES

The Edible Estates project proposes the replacement of the domestic front lawn with a highly productive edible landscape. Food grown in our front yards will connect us to the seasons, the organic cycles of the earth, and our neighbors. The banal lifeless space of uniform grass in front of the house will be replaced with the chaotic abundance of biodiversity. In becoming gardeners we will reconsider our connection to the land, what we take from it, and what we put in it. Each yard will be a unique expression of its location and of the inhabitant's desires.

OUR PLANET

Most of us feel like we don't any have any control over the direction in which our world is headed. As always, the newspapers are full of daily evidence for concern. Unlike the challenges of past generations, however, these struggles are no longer just local or broadly regional; they are an interlaced web of planetary challenges. How, then, do we respond in the face of the impossible scale of issues such as global energy production, climate change, and the related political aggressions and instabilities that accompany them? One thing we can do is act where we have influence, and in a capitalist society, that would be our private property. Here we have the freedom to create in some small measure the world in which we want to live.

OUR CLIMATE

We grow a lawn the same way anywhere in the world, but when we grow our own food we have to start paying attention to where we are. We experience our weather and climate in a personal way: they have a direct impact on us. The subtleties of sun, wind, air, and rain are meaningful.

OUR GOVERNMENT

A functioning democracy is predicated upon an informed populace of citizens who are in touch with each other. A democratic society suffers when people are physically out of touch. An Edible Estate can serve to stitch communities back together, taking a space that was previously isolating and turning it into a welcoming forum that reengages people with one another.

OUR CITY

There was a time when the effect of a town on the land around it was clearly in evidence within a radius of a few miles. For the most part the town depended on the materials, food, trades, and other resources that were available in the immediate region. The detritus of that consumption would stay within that same sphere of influence. Today the entire story of the impact of any city has become invisible because it is global. Cheap factory labor, foreign oil, circuitous water distribution systems, industrialized agriculture, and remote landfills all contribute to a general ignorance of the effects that daily human life has on the planet.

What happens when you graft agriculture onto a city? The more we keep ourselves in touch with the byproducts of our daily lives, the more we are reminded of how it is all connected. Edible Estates puts that evidence back in our cities and streets, back in our face.

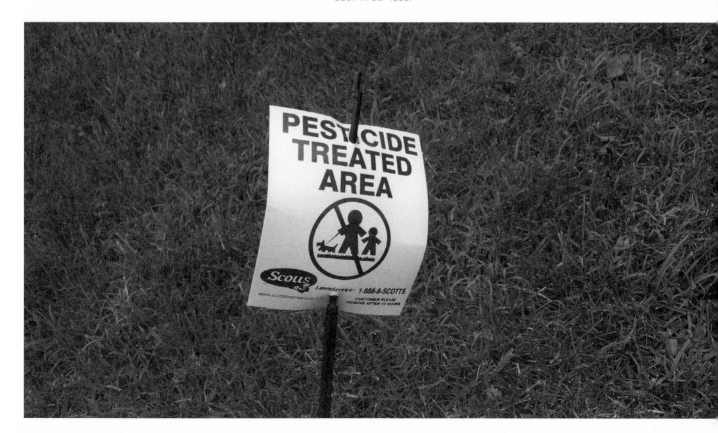

OUR STREET

Edible Estates gardens are meant to serve as provocations on the street. What happens when we share a street with one of these gardens? The front-yard gardeners become street performers for us. Coming out the door to tend their crops, they enact a daily ritual for the neighbors. We get to know them better than those who have lawns. We talk to them about how their crops are doing. They often can't eat everything they are growing, so they offer us the latest harvest of tomatoes or zucchini. We go out of our way to walk past the garden to see what is going on. Just the act of watching a garden grow can have a profound effect. When we observe as seeds sprout, plants mature, and fruit is produced, we can't help but be drawn in. We become witnesses, and are now complicit and a part of the story.

OUR NEIGHBORS

What happens when an Edibles Estate garden is not welcomed by the neighbors? Why do some people feel threatened by it? Anarchy, rodents, plummeting property values, willful self-expression, wild untamed nature, ugly decaying plants, and winter dormancy are some of the reasons that have been given. More to the point is a general sense that Edible Estate gardeners have broken some unspoken law of decency. Public tastes still favor conformity when it comes to the front yard, and any sort of deviation from the norm signals a social, if not moral, lapse. The abrupt appearance of such a garden on a street of endless lawns can be surprisingly shocking, but after the neighbors watch it grow in, they often come around. Perhaps the threats evoked by this wild intrusion into the neighborhood will eventually be a catalyst for questions. How far have we come from the core of our humanity that the act of growing our own food might be considered impolite, unseemly, threatening, radical, or even hostile?

OUR HOUSE

Private property, in particular the home, has become the geographic focus of our society. When we take stock of the standard American single-family residence, it becomes quite clear where the priorities are. It is within the walls of the house that the real investment and life of the residents occur. The land outside the walls typically receives much less attention, and can even become downright unwelcoming. Any activity in the yard will typically happen in back, where there is privacy. We are obsessed with our homes as protective bubbles from the realities around us. Today's towns and cities are engineered for isolation, and growing food in your front yard becomes a way to subvert this tendency. The front lawn, a highly visible slice of

private property, has the capacity also to be public. If we want to reintroduce a vital public realm into our communities, those with land and homes may ask what part of their private domain has public potential.

OUR DIRT

Just the act of spending an extended period of time outside with our hands in the dirt is a profoundly deviant act today! There is no rational or practical reason to do it. We can get anything we need at the store, right? The mortgage company refers to the physical house we live in as one of the "improvements" to the property. Pretty landscaping may be considered another improvement. But as far as the bank is concerned, the actual fertility and health of the dirt in our front yards has no economic value. Wouldn't it be great if a chemically contaminated lawn made a property impossible to sell, while organic gardening and thirty years of composting would dramatically increase our property values? Alas, today you can chart the exact economic stratum of any residential street based exclusively on the state of its chemically dependent front lawns.

OUR FOOD

In the process of making the Edible Estates gardens I have encountered some interesting reactions from people on the street. Some actually find it strange and a bit unseemly to ingest something that has grown in your yard. Yet most of us don't think twice before eating something grown under highly mysterious circumstances on the other side of the world. What you don't know can't hurt you; out of sight, out of mind. The act of eating is the moment in which we are most intimately connected to the world around us. We ingest into our bodies earthly matter that grew out of organic and environmental cycles happening all the time. We are all at the receiving end of dung and corpses decomposing, rainfall and evaporation, solar radiation, and so forth. What happens when the source of our food is far away and hidden from us? In moving food great distances, we pollute and expend precious energy, but perhaps more important, we lose visible evidence of our humble place in the big food chain.

OUR TIME

It is easy to romanticize gardening and food production when your life does not depend on what you are able to grow. An Edible Estate can be a lot of work! A lower-maintenance garden might be full of fruit trees and perennials well suited to your climate, but a more ambitious front yard might be full of annual vegetables and herbs that are rotated every season. Either way it demands a certain amount of dedication and time. Do we have enough time to grow our own food? Perhaps a better question is: How do we want to spend the little time that we do have? How about being outside with our family and friends, in touch with our neighbors, while watching with satisfaction as the plants we are tending begin to produce the healthiest local food to be found? It may be harder to defend the time we spend sitting in our cars or watching television.

But for those who just can't be bothered, what if all the front lawns on an entire street were turned over to urban farming teams? Each street would be lined in a series of diverse crops. The farmers would sell the produce and give what was left over to the families whose yards they tend. When buying a house, depending on your taste, you could decide if you wanted to live on artichoke avenue or citrus circle or radish road.

OUR MODEST MONUMENT

Edible Estates has no conventionally monumental intentions; it is a relatively small and modest intervention on our streets. The gardens are just beginning when they are planted and they continue to evolve. With just one season of neglect some gardens may disappear entirely. Politicians, architects, developers, urban citizens, we all crave permanent monuments that will give a sense of place and survive as a lasting testament to ourselves and our time. We were here! These monuments have their place, but their capacity to bring about meaningful change in the way we live is quite limited. A small garden of very modest means, humble materials, and a little effort can have a radical effect on the life of a family, how they spend their time and relate to their environment, whom they see, and how they eat. This singular local response to global issues can become a model. It can be enacted by anyone in the world and can have a monumental impact.

GROWING POWER: MILWAUKEE'S URBAN FARM

Will Allen

When Growing Power was founded a decade and a half ago, we developed a "Join hands around the globe" logo and the succinct motto, "Together We Are Growing Power," which we have stubbornly stuck to and adamantly guarded ever since. This positive message has been our brand, and my staff and I have worn that brand every day, whether we were working the farm, teaching a group of schoolchildren, or speaking to a gathering of community leaders.

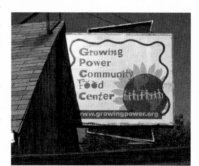

If you were to visit Growing Power today, though, you might, for the first time in our history, see me or several staff members sporting another uniform: a T-shirt or sweatshirt with a different logo and a new motto. The logo features a muscular, upraised arm and a hand clutching a batch of wriggling worms, and it says, "The Good Food Movement Is Now a Revolution."

Some of my colleagues and acquaintances, in what up to now has been called "the movement" toward local and sustainable agriculture, are a bit alarmed by this declaration. "Revolution" is a challenging word. Unlike a movement, which implies the gradual and methodical development of an idea or a set of ideas toward some ultimate but somewhat indefinite goal, a revolution implies a broad-based demand for rapid and perhaps irrevocable change with a firm and definite set of goals.

"Revolution" also can imply an unequivocal choice, a "with us or against us" mentality. It suggests the risk of putting all your cards on the table, one roll of the dice, now or never—and in the end, the possibility of having chosen the losing side.

But I did not declare this Good Food Revolution just to stir things up, and not to impose upon anyone the demand that they must join me or anyone else in immediately overturning the established social order—or, in this case, demolishing the industrialized agriculture system. Rather, I have come to believe that this revolution is simply a fact of the matter and of nature; it is a tide that can no longer be turned. I will even go so far as to say, without any sense of exaggeration, that I believe this revolution is already nearly won—won in the hearts and minds of a majority of people who say they want better food.

So, what is this revolution, where is it taking us, and what does it mean to say that it is inevitable? I have reached this conclusion, that we are now in a stage of revolution, over the course of the past year as I have gone from town to town, city to city, state to state, and nation to nation around the world, speaking about community farming and the future of food. Within this year I have seen larger and larger crowds and heard a louder and louder clamor for good food—meaning food that is safe, food that is wholly nutritious, food that is grown locally and sustainably so that we can know and trust its source and substance.

Moreover, I have seen a radical change in the makeup of this exploding audience. I am seeing and hearing not just from academics and small factions of local-food acolytes; I am constantly encountering people representative of every color, class, age, stratum of society, and walk of life. And all of them are demanding better access to better food.

That word, "demand," is like the word "revolution"—challenging and charged, confrontational. But looking long term, it is clear to me that this loud and clear demand will soon have to be heard in its economic sense, as in "the law of supply and. . . ."

It is fundamental to business that a market vacuum is abhorred and must be filled, and that supply will always rise to meet demand. What today might sound to agribusiness like a dangerous noise will tomorrow, upon further reflection, echo with the sweet music of opportunity. Herein lies the interesting irony of this revolution: We need not dismantle the Big Agriculture industry; we could not if we tried, if we remained only a lot

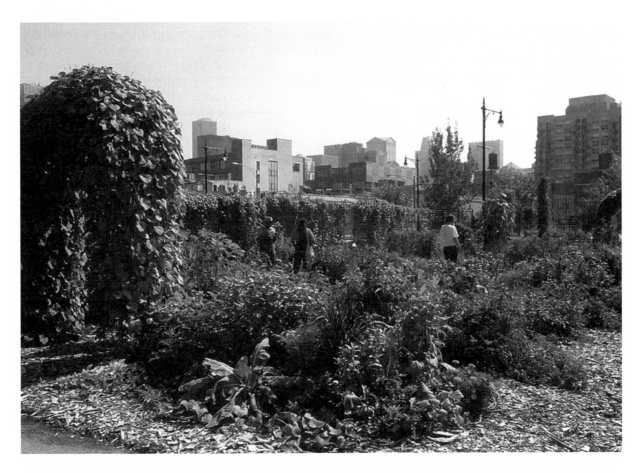

of individual voices crying in the wilderness. But Big Ag will willingly dismantle itself when it becomes clear that we, as large market forces, demand that it do so.

What, then, can we do to help enlighten the producers, processors, distributors, and sellers of food about the future we are writing for them? Before getting into that, I will say that much of that work, too, is already done or being done. I knew that the attention of the retail sector, where the market force is first felt, had become focused on the goals of the Good Food Revolution when Growing Power was approached by none other than Wal-Mart, which wanted to place our produce in its superstores. (Sadly, we could not accommodate them at the time; our two-acre urban farm didn't have quite the capacity to supply such a demand.)

I am also pleased to report that here in Milwaukee, at another mainstream supermarket, which is the single largest-selling supermarket location in the metro area, you can no longer buy any national brand of fresh chicken (you can still purchase frozen nuggets, "fingers," and pre-Buffaloed wings from who knows where). Instead, it sells chicken from a local Amish brand and from a Wisconsin free-range cooperative, which has adopted the clever slogans "Get Vocal about Local!" and "Do You Like the Sound of Local Drumsticks?"

I am well aware of how easy it is to claim "free-range"

status, and I do not know all the protocols of this producer, but at the least, this is a product raised and sold in Wisconsin, not shipped from Arkansas or Virginia, which scores points for energy sustainability. Moreover, this is clearly one very large retailer's response to what must have been a firm refusal by its clientele to continue to purchase cage-raised, water-processed, and possibly Salmonella-drenched chicken from distant mega-farms. I do not believe that this retailer came to the conclusion to exclude the unsustainable versus the sustainable based on anything other than market forces. Nevertheless, I am glad he or she did.

A few local anecdotes about market reforms do not a movement make, much less a revolution. But I am hearing similar stories everywhere I go these days, and it heartens me to think that day by day and quarter by fiscal quarter, the ledgers of large food retailers must be showing trends toward the local and the sustainable and away from the distant and the unsustainable.

So, to get back to the question at hand: Am I suggesting that nothing is left to be done, that in this revolution, it being already won, we haven't anything left to do but to wait for the bounty of better food to bestow itself upon us? By no means. There is much to be done and much for each one of us to do. As a very large group and as individuals, we must continue to press our food suppliers to provide accountability for our food sources, we must ourselves be accountable for investigating our food sources, and, when necessary, we must call to account those producers who do not measure up.

The greatest danger of winning this revolution too soon and too easily is that we will find ourselves being seduced by the blandishments of Big Ag with claims that it has become local when it has merely become slightly less distant; when it claims that it has become healthier by merely becoming a bit less dangerous; when it claims to have become sustainable when it has merely become marginally less exploitative of the land and the people who work it.

To bring about real and accountable results sooner, we have to each do a part to help those already on our side. We must support responsible growers by promoting them to retailers and support those retailers who have already moved or are moving toward responsibility. You can also join or expand a membership in a CSA (Community Supported Agriculture) with a known, responsible grower and start or patronize farmers' markets and co-ops that support local producers.

We can also do more with our own hands. Join or start a community garden with a neighborhood association or other community organization, for instance. And since the focus of this book is on what you can do on your own tract, your Edible Estate, let me say that I know no greater satisfaction than raising my own food on my own land. If you are willing to turn your acreage, your backyard, your patio, or even your front yard into a vegetable plot (even if it is in defiance of local ordinances or covenants), you may know that satisfaction, too.

Incongruously, the tragedies of the Great Depression and World War II proved the viability of local and home-based agriculture. During the Depression multitudes of farmers lost their lands or their crops to economic and natural forces, either to the devastating finality of foreclosure or to the crippling droughts that cruelly accompanied those years. Were it not for the native necessitousness of what was then still a largely rural citizenry, many would have starved. Then, during the war years, many farmers went off to fight, and those who remained had to provide not only for the home front but also for 16 million of our troops overseas and for England and the Soviet Union, our allies in that conflict. By the end of the war, more than 40 percent of the food produced in America came from backyard victory gardens, and much of the balance was going to the war effort. We were feeding ourselves, by ourselves.

We can do it again. Be forewarned, though. Small farming, alternative farming, and even home gardening involves inspiration, followed by perspiration, all too often ending in exasperation. I have my own home farm, a commercial operation to be sure, that I count on to provide not only food for me and my family but also an income to sustain us. In June

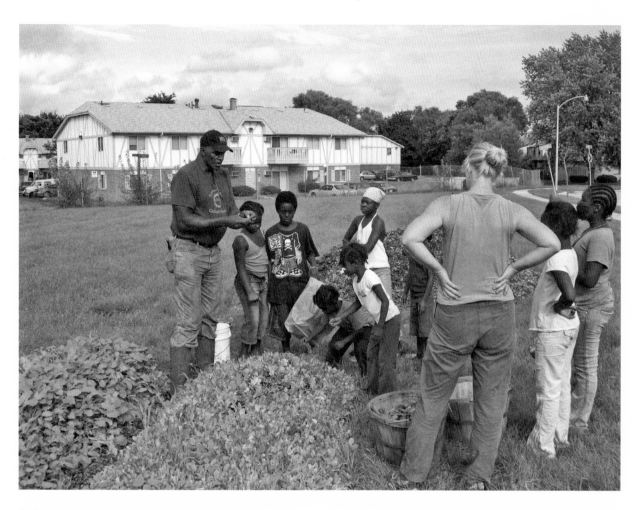

2009 all my crops were washed out in a tremendous flood, and all had to be replanted.

Fortunately, because I grow a great diversity of crops, I was able to replant with varieties I knew would be favored during the foreshortened season. I also had a reliable network of other growers who could readily fill the gaps for my customers during that unforeseen void. But I can tell you that I had more than a moment of deep concern for that season because it meant much to me and mine for the whole year. The lesson in this is that even if you have some space, time, and energy to devote to growing your own food, you will never know food security unless you become part of a local food system.

What is food security? And what is a local food system? They are interlocked. Food security is knowing that you have a reliable, year-round source of real nutrition. A local food system is a mechanism that ensures that security.

Almost no one, very few farmers even, attempts to grow all of the varieties of food he wants and needs, nor do many have the luxury of living in either a climate or a neighborhood that would allow it. It is well to believe that you are self-sufficient enough to go it alone, but it is better to know that you can make it together. Anyone can suffer a catastrophic loss, and for the single gardener that can be as large a catastrophe as a flood or hailstorm or as small as a single hungry woodchuck.

It is not enough, and you have not arrived at self-sufficiency, if a poor or damaged crop drives you back to the supermarket shelves, even though you may be lucky enough to afford to be there. If you are truly committed to Good Food and Good Food only, you need to be part of something larger than yourself—you need to be a part of a local food system. Such a system comes into being when enough producers, offering enough quality, quantity, and variety of foodstuffs to meet year-round consumer needs, form a co-op, a network, or a coalition capable of marketing and distributing their products as a significant proportion of the local food chain.

Right now in Milwaukee, the largest city in Wisconsin, a state that still has a highly diversified agriculture, only 1 percent of the food sold can be generously characterized as locally grown. This has come about because, for instance, we export enormous quantities of perfectly good Russet potatoes to distant places while importing equally enormous quantities of potatoes from Idaho and even Alaska. Why? Because consumers have been trained to believe that their potatoes are better than ours. It's the same with apples, carrots, and any number of crops that grow and store well right here in our heartland.

The revolution comes in breaking these long chains in the food system and in the minds of buyers and in building new, tight webs around the centers of communities. This involves little more than returning to the model that existed well into the last century, when practically every city and town in the nation served as, and had been founded as, the hub of a local market.

I see these webs beginning to grow—as with the Wisconsin chicken co-op mentioned above, in which 250 chicken farmers follow a single set of quality protocols—and it makes me optimistic that within a few years the 1 percent of local foods marketed here will have grown to 10 percent. That may still seem small proportionally, but the shift represents an order of magnitude in the right direction. To my mind that achievement will also represent a critical mass in demand that will keep things moving steadily in the right direction. And when it happens, and I do believe it will, we may be able to say that, yes, we have fomented a successful revolution.

But the campaign will not be over for me. My real revolution, the one that I spend most of my time advocating for and that I will continue to fight for long after these local food systems have become established for mainstream Americans, is to see that an equal opportunity to enjoy ready and reliable access to good food exists for all Americans, including all of those who have been marginalized out of the mainstream by unemployment and underemployment.

I cannot rest until, somehow, another form of the local food system I have been describing is also established and working in America's urban centers of poverty. I say another form because, unfortunately, the model will have to be different than it is for the mainstream. I know this because the economics of the existing food system are not working to bring fresh foods of even indifferent quality to these people, and there is no reason to think that the economics of better food will make it any more accessible to those who simply can't afford it. This, then, is the revolution for food security and food justice for all.

My Edible Estates, therefore, are schoolyards and vacant lots, abandoned tracts of brownfield land, any plot of any size and condition that can be used to grow food right in the middle of the community that needs it. It is a daunting prospect, to say the least, yet I am optimistic that I will see examples created in which these food deserts will be turned into oases where, again, at least 10 percent of the community's food needs will be supplied. I am optimistic about this not because I believe so strongly in my own abilities, but rather because, to my surprise, the people in those communities have been asking me for this opportunity since the day my journey as a farmer began.

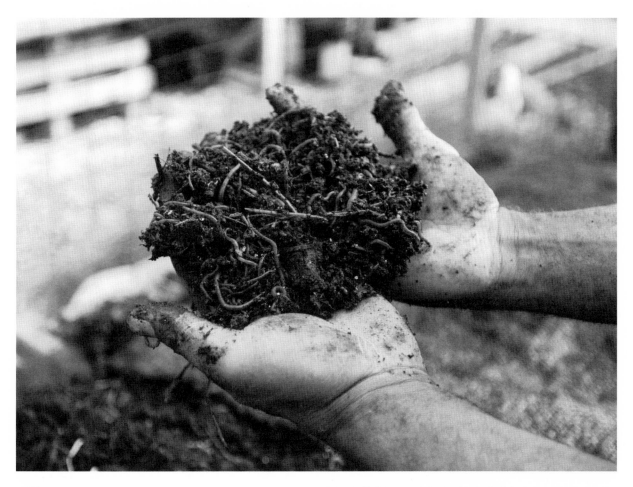

When I was born, my father was a sharecropper, but he wanted to free himself and his large family from that particular form of bondage. He saved enough to buy a small farm in Maryland. His market was the Washington, D.C., area, and it became focused on the large population of Southern blacks who were moving north and settling, people who were accustomed to having fresh produce in their diets but who expected it to be affordable.

I saw firsthand, by working with my hands, the amazing amount of produce that could be grown on just eight acres if the most intensive methods were used. Later, when I was living in Belgium and playing basketball, I got to know a number of farmers who also grew astonishing quantities of food on very small acreages by constantly enriching the soil with organic matter.

Eventually I was drawn back to farming, and in 1993 I bought a small roadside market and garden center on Milwaukee's impoverished north side. The stand was intended as a market for my own produce but also, and I hoped more importantly, as a place to offer fresher, more healthful food to an undernourished community. As it happened, that tiny two-acre plot, with its miniature storefront and handful of timeworn greenhouses, was the last tract of land within the city of Milwaukee that was still zoned for agriculture. It was almost as if some city planner had forgotten something—or that fate had somehow reserved the place for me. At any rate, I realized that I could do a good deal more at what I was then calling "Will's Roadside Produce Stand" than just sell vegetables from my farm. For one thing, I could grow more vegetables right there on site, and I proceeded to clear a half-acre bed, improve its soil, and plant it with an assortment of veggies.

Then something unexpected happened. I had hoped that this on-the-spot field would be a living, growing advertisement for the freshness of my farm fare. It turned out to be an even better advertisement for my farming methods. Children and young adults without other employment began to watch me at work. They would stand and stare as I cultivated a rich crop in the center of the city. Then they began to approach me, by ones and twos. "Mr. Allen," they might say, "your vegetables look so good. I've been trying to grow some peas and carrots in the backyard, but they don't do hardly anything. Can you show me how you do it?"

I was astounded. I had assumed that these young African-Americans of the urban North, two generations or more removed from roots similar to my own in the rural South, would have lost all contact with earth, water, and sun and all knowledge and interest in where and how their food was grown. I had figured it was up to me merely to provide better food than they were getting at the corner store, but here were children clamoring to learn how to grow food on their own to supplement their families' diets—and perhaps to satisfy some deep longing to reconnect with the cycles of nurturing life with work of the hands.

Nearly overnight I became a teacher as well as a farmer, demonstrating that simply scratching seeds into the hard clay of a city lot would not do. Good food starts with good soil, and so good soil must be grown first. Within just two years after I bought the last splinter of farmland in Milwaukee, Growing Power was born. It was incorporated as a nonprofit organization dedicated to teaching, training, and empowering communities to know and control their own food supplies. Today Growing Power is a national nonprofit and land trust with an international reach. The organization is involved in more than seventy partnership programs and projects in Milwaukee, across the nation, and around the globe, and we have trained thousands of people in our methods of intensive agriculture.

Yet I have to admit that it has taken a long time for these successes and those years of hard work to translate into the kind of impact I hoped for even in our own city. We helped hundreds, eventually thousands, toward food security and food justice, but there were always tens of thousands more in need, and poverty grew faster than we could find and plant new acres.

It pleases me to say, though, that the Good Food Revolution has now taken firm hold in this city, and in many other cities across the nation, in the exact place where it needed to happen most: the school cafeteria. Growing Power has been offered fifty new acres of public, urban land on which to grow food for a very hungry customer called the Milwaukee Public Schools. The district provides meals for 60,000 students each school day, and 76 percent of those children live below the poverty line. For some, the school meal is the only meal.

This is where the greatest impact can be made: among children whose developing minds and bodies need good food and who can learn lifelong good food habits. This is where we will be focusing our local efforts, and this is where we will develop the model for food security and food justice for all of urban America. This will be my Edible Estate and the landscape upon which true victory will be declared in the Good Food Revolution.

WHY MOW?
The Case Against Lawns

Michael Pollan

Anyone new to the experience of owning a lawn, as I am, soon figures out that there is more at stake here than a patch of grass. A lawn immediately establishes a certain relationship with one's neighbors and, by extension, the larger American landscape. Mowing the lawn, I realized the first time I gazed into my neighbor's yard and imagined him gazing back into mine, is a civic responsibility.

For no lawn is an island, at least in America. Starting at my front stoop, this scruffy green carpet tumbles down a hill and leaps across a one-lane road into my neighbor's yard. From there it skips over some wooded patches and stone walls before finding its way across a dozen other unfenced properties that lead down into the Housatonic Valley, there to begin its march south to the metropolitan area. Once below Danbury, the lawn—now purged of weeds and meticulously coiffed—races up and down the suburban lanes, heedless of property lines. It then heads west, crossing the New York border; moving now at a more stately pace, it strolls beneath the maples of Scarsdale, unfurls across a dozen golf courses, and wraps itself around the pale blue pools of Bronxville before pressing on toward the Hudson. New Jersey next is covered, an emerald postage stamp laid down front and back of ten thousand split-levels, before the broadening green river divides in two. One tributary pushes south, and does not pause until it has colonized the thin, sandy soils of Florida. The other dilates and spreads west, easily overtaking the Midwest's vast grid before running up against the inhospitable western states. But neither flinty soil nor obdurate climate will impede the lawn's march to the Pacific: it vaults the Rockies and, abetted by a monumental irrigation network, proceeds to green great stretches of western desert.

Nowhere in the world are lawns as prized as in America. In little more than a century, we've rolled a green mantle of grass across the continent, with scarcely a thought to the local conditions or expense. America has more than fifty

thousand square miles of lawn under cultivation, on which we spend an estimated $30 billion a year, according to the Lawn Institute, a Pleasant Hill, Tenn., outfit devoted to publicizing the benefits of turf to Americans (surely a case of preaching to the converted).

Like the interstate highway system, like fast-food chains, like television, the lawn has served to unify the American landscape; it is what makes the suburbs of Cleveland and Tucson, the streets of Eugene and Tampa, look more alike than not. According to Ann Leighton, the late historian of gardens, America has made essentially one important contribution to world garden design: the custom of "uniting the front lawns of however many houses there may be on both sides of a street to present an untroubled aspect of expansive green to the passer-by." France has its formal, geometric gardens, England its picturesque parks, and America this unbounded democratic river of manicured lawn along which we array our houses.

It is not easy to stand in the way of such a powerful current. Since we have traditionally eschewed fences and hedges in America (looking on these as Old World vestiges), the suburban

towered over the crew-cut lawns on either side of us and soon disturbed the peace of the entire neighborhood.

That subtle yet unmistakable frontier, where the closely shaved lawn rubs up against a shaggy one, is a scar on the face of suburbia, an intolerable hint of trouble in paradise. The scar shows up in *The Great Gatsby*, when Nick Carraway rents the house next to Gatsby's and fails to maintain his lawn according to West Egg standards. The rift between the two lawns so troubles Gatsby that he dispatches his gardener to mow Nick's grass and thereby erase it.

Our neighbors in Farmingdale displayed somewhat less class. "Lawn mower on the fritz?" they'd ask. "Want to borrow mine?" But the more heavily they leaned on my father, the more recalcitrant he became, until one summer, probably 1959 or '60, he let the lawn go altogether. The grass plants grew tall enough to flower and set seed; the lawn rippled in the breeze like a flag. There was beauty here, I'm sure, but it was not visible in this context. Stuck in the middle of a row of tract houses on Long Island, our lawn said turpitude rather than meadow, even though strictly speaking that is what it had become.

That summer I felt the hot breath of the majority's tyranny for the first

vista can be marred by the negligence—or dissent—of a single property owner. This is why lawn care is regarded as such an important civic responsibility in the suburbs, and why the majority will not tolerate the laggard. I learned this at an early age, growing up in a cookie-cutter subdivision in Farmingdale, Long Island.

My father, you see, was a lawn dissident. Whether owing to laziness or contempt for his neighbors I was never sure, but he could not see much point in cranking up the Toro more than once a month or so. The grass on our quarter-acre plot

time. No one said anything now, but you could hear it all the same: Mow your lawn or get out. Certain neighbors let it be known to my parents that I was not to play with their children. Cars would slow down as they drove by. Probably some of the drivers were merely curious: they saw the unmowed lawn and wondered if someone had left in a hurry, or perhaps died. But others drove by in a manner that was unmistakably expressive, slowing down as they drew near and then hitting the gas angrily as they passed—pithy driving, the sort of move that is second nature to a Klansman.

We got the message by other media, too. Our next-door neighbor, a mild engineer who was my father's last remaining friend in the development, was charged with the unpleasant task of conveying the sense of community to my father. It was early on a summer evening that he came to deliver his message. I don't remember it all (I was only four or five at the time), but I can imagine him taking a highball glass from my mother, squeaking out what he had been told to say about the threat to property values and then waiting for my father—who next to him was a bear—to respond.

My father's reply could not have been more eloquent. Without a word he strode out to the garage and cranked up the rusty old Toro for the first time since fall; it's a miracle the thing started. He pushed it out to the curb and then started back across the lawn to the house, but not in a straight line: he swerved right, then left, then right again. He had cut an "S" in the high grass. Then he made an "M," and finally a "P." These are his initials, and as soon as he finished writing them he wheeled the lawn mower back to the garage, never to start it up again.

I wasn't prepared to take such a hard line on my new lawn, at least not right off. So I bought a lawn mower, a Toro, and started mowing. Four hours every Saturday. At first I tried for a kind of Zen approach, clearing my mind of everything but the task at hand, immersing myself in the lawn-mowing here-and-now. I liked the idea that my weekly sessions with the grass would acquaint me with the minutest details of my yard. I soon knew by heart the exact location of every stump and stone, the tunnel route of each resident mole, the address of every anthill.

I noticed that where rain collected white clover flourished, that it was on the drier rises that crabgrass thrived. After a few weekends I had a map of the lawn in my head as precise and comprehensive as the mental map one has to the back of his hand.

The finished product pleased me, too, the fine scent and the sense of order restored that a new-cut lawn exhales. My house abuts woods on two sides, and mowing the lawn is, in both a real and metaphorical sense, how I keep the forest at bay and preserve my place in this landscape. Much as we've come to distrust it, the urge to dominate nature is a deeply human one, and lawn mowing answers to it. I thought of the lawn mower as civilization's knife and my lawn as the hospitable plane it carved out of the wilderness. My lawn was a part of nature made fit for human habitation.

So perhaps the allure of lawns is in the genes. The sociobiologists think so: they've gone so far as to propose a "Savanna Syndrome" to explain our fondness for grass. Encoded in our DNA is a preference for an open grassy landscape resembling the short-grass savannas of Africa on which we evolved and spent our first few million years. This is said to explain why we have remade the wooded landscapes of Europe and North America in the image of East Africa.

Such theories go some way toward explaining the widespread appeal of grass, but they don't really account for the American Lawn. They don't, for instance, account for the keen interest Jay Gatsby takes in Nick Carraway's lawn, or the scandal my father's lawn sparked in Farmingdale. Or the fact that, in America, we have taken down our fences and hedges in order to combine our lawns. And they don't even begin to account for the unmistakable odor of virtue that hovers in this country over a scrupulously maintained lawn.

If any individual can be said to have invented the American lawn, it is Frederick Law Olmsted. In 1868 he received a commission to design Riverside, outside of Chicago, one of

the first planned suburban communities in America. Olmsted's design stipulated that each house be set back thirty feet from the road and it proscribed walls. He was reacting against the "high dead-walls" of England, which he felt made a row of homes there seem "as of a series of private madhouses." In Riverside, each owner would maintain one or two trees and a lawn that would flow seamlessly into his neighbors', creating the impression that all lived together in a single park.

Olmsted was part of a generation of American landscape designer-reformers who set out at midcentury to beautify the American landscape. That it needed beautification may seem surprising to us today, assuming as we do that the history of the landscape is a story of decline, but few at the time thought otherwise. William Cobbett, visiting from England, was struck at the "out-of-door slovenliness" of American homesteads. Each farmer, he wrote, was content with his "shell of boards, while all around him is as barren as the sea beach—though there is no English shrub, or flower, which will not grow and flourish here."

The land looked as if it had been shaped and cleared in a great hurry, as indeed it had: the landscape largely denuded of trees, makeshift fences outlining badly plowed fields, tree stumps everywhere one looked. As Cobbett and many other nineteenth-century visitors noted, hardly anyone practiced ornamental gardening; the typical yard was "landscaped" in the style Southerners would come to call "white trash": a few chickens, some busted farm equipment, mud and weeds, an unkempt patch of vegetables.

This might do for farmers, but for the growing number of middle-class city people moving to the "borderland" in the years following the Civil War, something more respectable was called for. In 1870 Frank J. Scott, seeking to make Olmsted's ideas accessible to the middle class, published the first volume ever devoted to "suburban home embellishment": *The Art of Beautifying Suburban Home Grounds*, a book that probably did more than any other to determine the look of the suburban landscape in America. Like so many reformers of his time, Scott was nothing if not sure of himself: "A smooth, closely shaven surface of grass is by far the most essential element of beauty on the grounds of a suburban house."

Americans like Olmsted and Scott did not invent the lawn; lawns had been popular in England since Tudor times. But in England, lawns were usually found only on estates; the Americans democratized them, cutting the vast manorial greenswards into quarter-acre slices everyone could afford. Also, the English never considered the lawn an end in itself:

it served as a setting for lawn games and as a backdrop for flowerbeds and trees. Scott subordinated all other elements of the landscape to the lawn; flowers were permissible, but only on the periphery of the grass: "Let your lawn be your home's velvet robe, and your flowers its not too promiscuous decoration."

But Scott's most radical departure from Old World practice was to dwell on the individual's responsibility to his neighbors. "It is unchristian," he declared, "to hedge from the sight of others the beauties of nature which it has been our good fortune to create or secure." One's lawn, Scott held, should contribute to the collective landscape. "The beauty obtained by throwing front grounds open together, is of that excellent quality which enriches all who take part in the exchange, and makes no man poorer." Like Olmsted before him, Scott sought to elevate an unassuming patch of turfgrass into an institution of democracy.

With our open-faced front lawns we declare our like-mindedness to our neighbors—and our distance from the English, who surround their yards with "inhospitable brick wall, topped with broken bottles," to thwart the envious gaze of the lower orders. The American lawn is an egalitarian conceit, implying that there is no reason to hide behind fence or hedge since we all occupy the same middle class. We are all property owners here, the lawn announces, and that suggests its other purpose: to provide a suitably grand stage for the proud display of one's own house. Noting that our yards were organized "to capture the admiration of the street," one garden writer in 1921 attributed the popularity of open lawns to our "infantile instinct to cry 'hello!' to the passer-by, to lift up our possessions to his gaze."

Of course, the democratic front yard has its darker, more coercive side, as my family learned in Farmingdale. In specifying the "plain style" of an unembellished lawn for American front yards, the midcentury designer-reformers were, like Puritan ministers, laying down rigid conventions governing our relationship to the land, our observance of which would henceforth be taken as an index of our character. And just as the Puritans would not tolerate any individual who sought to establish his or her own back-channel relationship with the divinity, the members of the suburban utopia do not tolerate the homeowner who establishes a relationship with the land that is not mediated by the group's conventions.

The parallel is not as farfetched as it might sound, when you recall that nature in America has often been regarded as divine. Think of nature as Spirit, the collective suburban lawn as the Church, and lawn mowing as a kind of sacrament. You begin to see why ornamental gardening would take so long to catch on

in America, and why my father might seem an antinomian in the eyes of his neighbors. Like Hester Prynne, he claimed not to need their consecration for his actions; perhaps his initials in the front lawn were a kind of Emerald Letter.

Possibly because it is this common land, rather than race or tribe, that makes us all Americans, we have developed a deep distrust of individualistic approaches to the landscape. The land is too important to our identity as Americans to simply allow everyone to have his own way with it. And once we decide that the land should serve as a vehicle of consensus, rather than an arena of self-expression, the American lawn—collective, national, ritualized, and plain—begins to look inevitable.

After my first season of lawn mowing, the Zen approach began to wear thin. I had taken up flower and vegetable gardening, and soon came to resent the four hours that my lawn demanded of me each week. I tired of the endless circuit, pushing the howling mower back and forth across the vast page of my yard, recopying the same green sentences over and over: "I am a conscientious homeowner. I share your middle-class values."

Lawn care was gardening aimed at capturing "the admiration of the street," a ritual of consensus I did not have my heart in. I began to entertain idle fantasies of rebellion: Why couldn't I plant a hedge along the road, remove my property from the national stream of greensward and do something else with it?

The third spring I planted fruit trees in the front lawn—apple, peach, cherry, and plum—hoping these would relieve the monotony and begin to make the lawn productive. Behind the house, I put in a perennial border. I built three raised beds out of old chestnut barnboards and planted two dozen different vegetable varieties. Hard work though it was, removing the grass from the site of my new beds proved a keen pleasure. First I outlined the beds with string. Then I made an incision in the lawn with the sharp edge of a spade. Starting at one end, I pried the sod from the soil and slowly rolled it up like a carpet. The grass made a tearing sound as I broke its grip on the earth. I felt a little like a pioneer subduing the forest with his ax; I daydreamed of scalping the entire yard. But I didn't do it; I continued to observe front-yard conventions, mowing assiduously and locating all my new garden beds in the backyard.

The more serious about gardening I became, the more dubious lawns seemed. The problem for me was not, as it was for my father, the relation to my neighbors that a lawn implied; it was the lawn's relationship to nature. For however democratic a lawn may be with respect to one's neighbors, with respect to nature it is authoritarian. Under the mower's brutal indiscriminate rotor, the landscape is subdued, homogenized, dominated utterly. I became convinced that lawn care had about as much to do with gardening as floor waxing, or road paving. Gardening was a subtle process of give and take with the landscape, a search for some middle ground between culture and nature. A lawn was nature under culture's boot.

Mowing the lawn, I felt like I was battling the earth rather than working it; each week it sent forth a green army and each week I beat it back with my infernal machine. Unlike every other plant in my garden, the grasses were anonymous, massified, deprived of any change or development whatsoever, not to mention any semblance of self-determination. I ruled a totalitarian landscape.

Hot monotonous hours behind the mower gave rise to existential speculations. I spent part of one afternoon trying to decide who, in the absurdist drama of lawn mowing, was

Sisyphus. Me? A case could certainly be made. Or was it the grass, pushing up through the soil every week, one layer of cells at a time, only to be cut down and then, perversely, encouraged (with fertilizer, lime, etc.) to start the whole doomed process over again? Another day it occurred to me that time as we know it doesn't exist in the lawn, since grass never dies or is allowed to flower and set seed. Lawns are nature purged of sex and death. No wonder Americans like them so much.

And just where was my lawn, anyway? The answer's not as obvious as it seems. Gardening, I had come to appreciate, is a painstaking exploration of place; everything that happens in my garden—the thriving and dying of particular plants, the maraudings of various insects and other pests—teaches me to know this patch of land intimately, its geology and microclimate, the particular ecology of its local weeds and animals and insects. My garden prospers to the extent I grasp these particularities and adapt to them.

Lawns work on the opposite principle. They depend for their success on the overcoming of local conditions. Like Jefferson superimposing one great grid over the infinitely various topography of the Northwest Territory, we superimpose our lawns on the land. And since the geography and climate of much of this country

are poorly suited to turfgrasses (none of which is native), this can't be accomplished without the tools of twentieth-century industrial civilization—its chemical fertilizers, pesticides, herbicides, and machinery. For we won't settle for the lawn that will grow here; we want the one that grows there, that dense springy supergreen and weed-free carpet, that Platonic ideal of a lawn we glimpse in the ChemLawn commercials, the magazine spreads, the kitschy sitcom yards, the sublime links and pristine diamonds. Our lawns exist less here than there; they drink from the national stream of images, lift our gaze from the real places where we live and fix it on unreal places elsewhere. Lawns are a form of television.

Need I point out that such an approach to "nature" is not likely to be environmentally sound? Lately we have begun to recognize that we are poisoning ourselves with our lawns, which receive, on average, more pesticide and herbicide per acre than just about any crop grown in this country. Suits fly against the national lawn-care companies, and interest is kindled in "organic" methods of lawn care. But the problem is larger than this. Lawns, I am convinced, are a symptom of, and a metaphor for, our skewed relationship to the land. They teach us that, with the help of petrochemicals and technology, we can bend nature to our will. Lawns stoke our hubris with regard to the land. What is the alternative? To turn them into gardens. I'm not suggesting that there is no place for lawns in these gardens or that gardens by themselves will right our relationship to the land, but the habits of thought they foster can take us some way in that direction.

Gardening, as compared to lawn care, tutors us in nature's ways, fostering an ethic of give and take with respect to the land.

Gardens instruct us in the particularities of place. They lessen our dependence on distant sources of energy, technology, food, and, for that matter, interest.

For if lawn mowing feels like copying the same sentence over and over, gardening is like writing out new ones, an infinitely variable process of invention and discovery. Gardens also teach the necessary if rather un-American lesson that nature and culture can be compromised, that there might be some middle ground between the lawn and the forest, between those who would complete the conquest of the planet in the name of

progress, and those who believe it's time we abdicated our rule and left the earth in the care of its more innocent species. The garden suggests there might be a place where we can meet nature half way.

Probably you will want to know if I have begun to practice what I'm preaching. Well, I have not ripped out my lawn entirely. But each spring larger and larger tracts of it give way to garden. Last year I took a half acre and planted a meadow of black-eyed Susans and oxeye daisies. In return for a single annual scything,

I am rewarded with a field of flowers from May until frost.

The lawn is shrinking, and I've hired a neighborhood kid to mow what's left of it. Any Saturday that Bon Jovi, Twisted Sister, or Van Halen isn't playing the Hartford Civic Center, this large blond teen-aged being is apt to show up with a forty-eight-inch John Deere mower that shears the lawn in less than an hour. It's thirty dollars a week, but he's freed me from my dark musings about the lawn and so given me more time in the garden.

Out in front, along the road where my lawn overlooks my neighbors', and in turn the rest of the country's, I have made my most radical move. I built a split-rail fence and have begun to plant a hedge along it, a rough one made up of forsythia, lilac, bittersweet, and bridal wreath. As soon as this hedge grows tall and thick, my secession from the national lawn will be complete.

Anything then is possible. I could let it all revert to meadow, or even forest, except that I don't go in for that sort of self-effacement. I could put in a pumpkin patch, a lily pond, or maybe an apple orchard. And I could even leave an area of grass. But even if I did, this would be a very different lawn from the one I have now. For one thing, it would have a frame, which means it could accommodate plants more subtle and various than the screaming marigolds, fierce red salvias, and musclebound rhododendrons that people usually throw into the ring against a big unfenced lawn. Walled off from the neighbors, no longer a tributary of the national stream, my lawn would now form a distinct and private space—become part of a garden, rather than a substitute for one.

Yes, there might well be a place for a small lawn in my new garden. But I think I'll wait until the hedge fills in before I make a decision. It's a private matter, and I'm trying to keep politics out of it.

THE GREAT GRID

Lesley Stern

San Diego is an American city and the gardens of San Diego are American gardens. My street, which is not really my street nor anyone else's either, is like any other street in San Diego, and thus like any other street in America.

Herman Avenue runs in a straight line for about ten blocks, between University and Thorn. If you stand at one end and cast your eye down the avenue, you can almost see the other end. Or at least you can imagine yourself master of all you survey. Like a fish caught on the end of a line, your eye is drawn through space, down the asphalt, its passage smoothly dissecting the modest expanse of lawns on either side of the street. You would be right not to expect any major surprises, any tricky turns or crooked deviations from the straight and narrow. For this is an American street, lined by American gardens. As you proceed down the street you will see few people in any of the front yards bordering it, scarcely any signs of labor. One lawn seemingly flows into the next, and the palm trees, planted on the verge, provide continuity, creating the sense of a vista.

Yet Herman Avenue isn't entirely successful in its aspirations to American typicality. It falls short of the mark because of its length. It should, to be properly typical, run from one end of the town (or at least the suburb) to the other. One reason for its relative shortness is that at Thorn it runs into a canyon. All over San Diego straight lines terminate in canyons. Sometimes, defeated by topography, roads simply terminate without warning or explanation. But often there is a struggle between the sovereignty of the grid and canyonic eccentricity. That is when interesting things happen to streets and, by pragmatic extrapolation, to gardens. As the terrain squiggles (around various bays as well as canyons), so

gardens evolve unpredictably, erratically defined, with dubious boundaries. In other instances boundaries are obsessively instituted—in gated communities, particularly, and in wealthy exurbanite properties, positioned between the city and the wilderness. But mostly the grid prevails.

In Sydney, which is not a rationally gridded city, I am forever getting lost, I never know where I am, and this is the charm of the place. But in America you can always orient yourself according to north, south, east, and west. This is not charming (even though it does save time) and neither is it orienting. It merely produces the *sense* of orientation, the mistaken but indelibly inscribed and peculiarly American sense of arriving. Sometimes when I ask directions from an American and he obliges with an unerring sense of direction (head west on A, and take the 5 North to the 8 East, and so on) I feel incapacitated by my own bodily topography, the mess of an imploded musculature, spaghettied veins, and scrambled memory. I look at him, beaming with earnest helpfulness, and see American civic virtue mapped over his body in the form of a grid. This sense of rectitude, of straight lines intersecting at right angles: he has it in him. He is a walking, talking, living grid.

The great grid conceived of by Thomas Jefferson through the National Land Survey and worked into the Land Ordinance Act of 1785 was of fundamental importance in inaugurating an American concept of social space. Social space in this country has a cartographic foundation, and so, too, does its democracy. The National Survey extended over nearly three-quarters of the surface of the North American continent. The land, assumed as a carte blanche, was divided up into democratic parcels (farms initially, of an equal size), the parcels were linked by a gridded road system, roads cut through the countryside leading to townships, which were organized in a square. Eventually suburbs developed on the grid model. Houses (each family allotted its own detached yard with a house in the middle) faced onto the street, unbounded by walls or gates, each with a lawn, and on the so-called "nature strip" between the pedestrian walkway and the street proper, an avenue of trees.

Jefferson's divisions were motivated by an impulse of democratic rationality—for all "liberty, a farmyard wide"—and this division of land was intended to create a new and more perfect society. The grid (in contrast to, say, the Baroque city, in which lines emanated from a single point of power) was intended to distribute power equally across space. It is also out of this impulse of democratic rationality that the various city ordinances have grown that proscribe walled gardens, and which ensure a sweep of continuous shaven green.

And if you are one of the lucky ones, lucky enough to own a modest property fronting the street, then you somehow absorb the notion, sprinkled into your being by the Great Big Sprinkler in the Sky (just as the lawn absorbs monthly doses of fertilizer distributed through the automatic sprinkler system), that you own not only a house and garden but democracy as well. Of course, people do not stand on their lawns like garden gnomes saying, Welcome to my home and garden and my democracy. But just as house and garden go together like a horse and carriage, so do America and democracy; to many Americans the term "American democracy" is a naturalized condensation. To many other people in the world it is a tautology.

Jefferson was the architect not only of the Land Ordinance Act—which, incidentally, also made provision for public space dedicated to parks and schools—but also of that founding document of the American democratic tradition, the Declaration of Independence. It was he who wrote, famously, "We hold these truths to be self-evident, that all men are created equal, that they are endowed by their creator with certain unalienable rights, that among these are life, liberty, and the pursuit of happiness." But as of 1776 most African-Americans lived in slavery, and, in any case, each was counted in the Constitution itself not as a person but as three-fifths of a whole person—which could only be, for purposes of citizenship, a white man. The various Indian tribes and nations were excluded from many unalienable rights, as were all women, who could not vote.

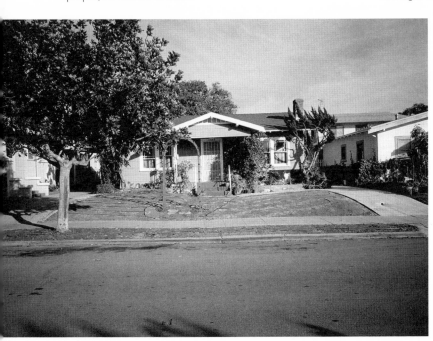

In addition to being a statesman, Jefferson was an extraordinarily inventive and experimental farmer and gardener, importing and distributing seeds through a vast range of international and national contacts. His garden at Monticello has been described as his "Ellis Island of immigrant vegetables." Often, as I toil in the vegetable garden, I brood malevolently on Jefferson, thinking about how his immigrant vegetables got a better deal than his gardeners, for magnificent Monticello was built on the labor of slaves. I also muse on the fact that Monticello itself escaped the democratic grid; if anything it was designed against the constraints of the grid and in imitation of those eighteenth-century landscape painters and English landscape architects who were attempting to reproduce a sense of the picturesque in reaction against earlier more rigid and formal designs.

Pulling weeds, I ponder the strangeness of American democracy. To say American democracy is built on a grid is one thing. Can we also say it is built on slavery? Certainly it is the case that the three-fifths clause, initially introduced into the Constitution as a taxation measurement, was exploited by the slave states as a condition for their joining the Union, because it upped the number of seats they had in Congress. In the crucial election of 1800 (a tipping point in American history because it signaled the demise of Federalist domination of the government and the advent of Republican rule), if Jefferson had not had the slave count, he would not have won. Twelve to fourteen votes, gained by virtue of people who were themselves denied the vote, were given to the Southern candidate no matter what.

I came to live in America, more precisely, in San Diego, in July 2000. For ten years prior to this I had lived in an apartment in Bondi Beach, Sydney, marvelously close to the ocean but without a garden. On a Sunday afternoon in November 2000 I walked in a desultory manner into the empty house for sale on Herman Avenue, an unremarkable house from the street with a front yard like every other—a shabby brownish lawn, two ugly junipers coated in dust, a gray concrete path dissecting the yard, running in a straight line from porch to pavement. On the nature strip there was a lumpy carrot tree, but scattered down the avenue there were the obligatory palm trees. When I came to San Diego I decided I would like to live in North Park, mainly because of its languid airs and graces; it felt as though for the last fifty years it had been on the verge of gentrification, always almost but never quite arriving. More to the point, I could just about afford a mortgage here. I rather liked the utter typicality of this house and garden, but had no expectations. The neighboring garden, however, was an inspiration. The gardener, whom I would subsequently come to know as Mrs. Tam, was growing squash all along the front of the house, green tentacles spread over her lawn, reaching down onto the walkway ready to snare passersby, suck their souls, and turn them into pumpkins.

As I opened the front door I could see through the house, through a series of windows, onto a backyard dominated by three huge, old, sprawling trees. Walking into the backyard I saw in the rear of the property an abandoned plot overrun with weeds. In an instant I projected onto the landscape a verdant vegetable garden. Coming back into the house I sensed its history and felt an affinity; it felt right. And as I walked back out onto the street my eyes stripped the front yard, peeling back the lawn, chucking every blade of grass. In my mind's eye I saw a garden, a raucous, tumbling, jam-packed flower garden. On the 1st of January 2001 we moved into Herman Avenue, and before unpacking any boxes I cleared a small space of weeds in the back corner and sowed a lettuce mix.

In between my arrival in the U.S. and moving into Herman Avenue, there was an election in this country uncannily ghosted by the election held two hundred years earlier. Again the Democrats were ousted, and the Republicans took office although their victory was determined by a dubious vote count. The state where the corruption was most pronounced was a Southern state, Florida, and the voters who were most disenfranchised and cheated were African-Americans. In 1858 the abolitionist Theodore Parker (a persistent critic of Jefferson), discussing the way the nation was made almost mute on the subject of slavery, said, "The Democratic hands of America have sewed up her own mouth with an iron thread."

As I rip up the lawn and plant purple sage and yellow roses and pink and white billowing gaura and a tiny fig tree and an Australian blue hibiscus and a lemon and a peach tree, I ponder these words—their relevance to history and their pertinence today. I wonder how I will live in this strange land. In gardening I enact something of an answer: I will live in this country precisely by gardening. Ripping up the lawn is a beginning, a small gesture of defiance against the grid. But it is also a way of messing with the border between the private and the public, of entering that zone where the domestic encounters the foreign. Traipsing down the garden path I begin to study the local climate, the availability of species, the disappearance and preservation of plants, the management of water and fire in this desert region. A variety of historical trajectories and arcane anecdotal threads emerges, linking San Diego to a larger landscape, linking gardening to other decidedly less domestic topoi.

Later I read Jefferson's letters and Garden and Farm Books, and am struck by his constant yearning for "riddance from public cares" so that he can devote himself to growing things. "No occupation is so delightful to me as the culture of the earth, and no culture comparable to that of the garden," he writes. "The greatest service which can be rendered any country is to add a useful plant to its culture." I am jolted into a moment's empathy with old man Jefferson. I will continue, as an alien, to muse malevolently, and to remember that every garden has a domestic history that links it to a nation's history. Ripping up the lawn does not, I know, remove this puny patch of earth from the grid of rationality. But a garden, any garden, is also a place where you can make another country; it is a place of irrationality, an imaginary place.

MY HOUSE
IN THE GARDEN

Rosalind Creasy

You could say that my house is nestled in a garden, although merely calling it a garden belies its true importance. It's really an ever-changing suburban statement. On any given day in spring I might harvest sweet crunchy snap peas and an amazing salad of wild greens for supper, and give a neighbor a dozen freshly laid eggs. In early summer I might photograph beneficial insects on the wheat, pick a huge bouquet of roses, and invite the neighborhood children in to pick strawberries. Yet my garden has not always been so bountiful and people-friendly.

Nearly forty years ago my family and I moved into our house in the San Francisco Bay area, where I inherited a shady back-yard and a front yard that was mostly lawn. Because of the shade I couldn't grow vegetables in the back. The front yard was my only option, but since there seemed to be an unwritten law against vegetables in a suburban front yard at the time, I felt I could only get away with sneaking a few basil and pepper plants into the flowerbeds. As my interest in gardening grew, the lawn shrank proportionately. People were complimenting the front garden, so each season I became bolder and devoted more of the space to edibles.

The biggest change to the front yard came in 1985, when I began working on my book *Cooking from the Garden*, which was about edible theme gardens and their beautiful and flavorful harvests. I wanted to create a trial garden for at least a hundred varieties of vegetables that few gardeners had seen back then, such as yellow or red carrots and all-blue potatoes. As an early supporter of the Seed Savers Exchange, I felt strongly that there was an urgent need to save the thousands of heirloom vegetable varieties that were going extinct, and the only way to do that was to sing their praises (especially the succulent thin-skinned tomatoes and melting-fleshed melons) to the public in general as well as to food professionals.

From my years of gardening I knew that not all of the old open-pollinated vegetable varieties were great, so I wanted to grow out the most promising of the unusual tomatoes, squash, and other edibles to make sure they tasted good. I also knew that some were very prone to disease, while others were awkward looking and didn't fit into an edible landscape. I felt it was important to examine these unusual vegetables, herbs, and edible flowers firsthand. I needed to grow examples of them in various themes to photograph, and I needed to have them at my fingertips so I could develop recipes that showcased their unique qualities. And I wanted to grow the garden completely organically. (Up until then my gardens had been mostly organic, but by default; at that point it became a conscious decision.)

Keeping all this in mind, I hired an experienced food gardener for what was to be a two-year project. With a lot of help we dug up the entire front yard, added truckloads of organic matter to the heavy clay soil, and transformed the front yard into a series of garden beds. Little did I know where it would all lead. At first the book project was quite intellectual and solitary. I sought out seeds, we planted them, and I photographed the plants and kept notes during the entire process. Just as I hoped, we grew out hundreds of wonderful annual edibles and mini-vegetable gardens with Mexican, French, German, Native American, herb, salad, and Asian themes.

I soon discovered that by nature, gardening in the front yard is a communal experience. I never knew who might stop and share a garden-inspired story with me when I was in the garden. One day, when the lettuces were large enough to be identified, a woman who was on her morning jog paused to tell me about her mother's garden in France that had the same lettuces, and asked where she could get seeds for these memorable varieties. Another time a fellow who was paving the road was thrilled to see my purple gomphrena because it was a plant his grandmother had grown. So I gave him some flowery seed heads to take home.

Throughout the growing season I had discouraged the neighborhood children from coming into the garden because I was afraid they might step on plants or pick something I was about to photograph. Yet, as the harvest began, some of the adults became involved. A woman, who had lived in Germany and loved to cook, suggested that I add some of my savory every time I cooked beans. One neighbor, who was from Taiwan, gave me her mother's recipe for pickled Chinese cabbage, while another who had lived in France offered to test French recipes for me! At this point I added a birdbath to the area and I noticed that there were more birds in the garden. And the kids kept hanging around to see what was going on.

When my book project was complete, I kept the garden going another year because I had been asked to write a syndicated column for the *Los Angeles Times* on unusual vegetables. Since

I couldn't buy purple broccoli, Cinderella pumpkins, Brandywine tomatoes, edible flowers, and such, I needed to grow them so I could photograph them in their garden glory, create and test more recipes, and photograph the delectable dishes. After two years of adding organic matter to the beds, the garden was in great shape and the plants were growing very well. But since this was a new writing and photography gig, I had to make my new photos look different from those I had taken the first few years. So we moved a pile of used brick I had squirreled away

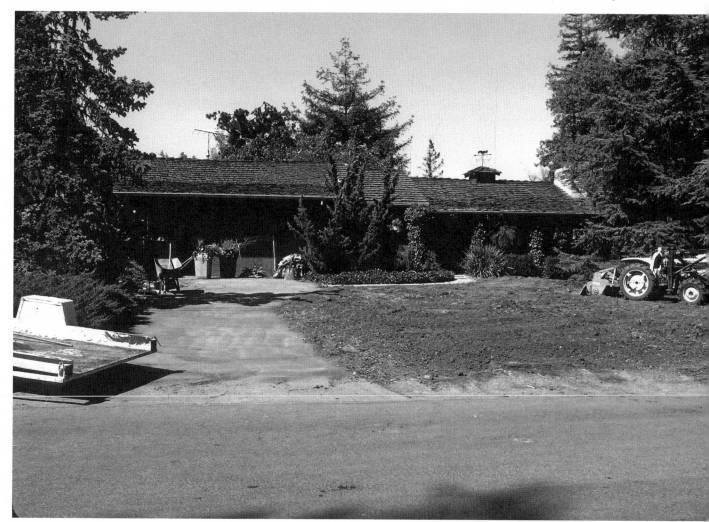

in the backyard, made formal paths, and added an arbor. And the kids kept hanging around.

The following year the book finally came out, and I needed the garden yet again: *CNN Headline News* had lined up a story on heirloom vegetables; *CBS This Morning* had requested a story on growing mesclun salad greens in the front yard; and the *New York Times* wanted an article on cooking with unusual vegetables and planned to come photograph my garden. Suddenly I was off on a new path in my career that I hadn't anticipated. And the kids were still watching and waiting.

As you've been reading these garden memoirs, you've probably guessed what happened next. By the end of the third summer, I figured that since we were going to take out the whole garden and put in a new one for winter, why not let some of the neighborhood kids in this time? They could pull carrots that were ready to come out of the ground and pick flowers until they dropped. I spoke with their parents and arranged for four children between the ages of six and twelve to have at it. Well, they really got into it. They picked hundreds of gomphrena, cosmos, nasturtium, zinnia, and statice flowers, and put them in baskets. (I admit that it was hard for me, but I restrained myself and didn't tell them to only pick long stems because otherwise they wouldn't fit into vases, or to avoid the old heads as they only last a day.) So, they cut two-inch stems and three-inch stems, and six-inch stems—whatever they wanted. This went on for two hours, at which point they all took off for one of their front lawns, laid out the flowers, and proceeded to sort them. Each child went to his or her own house and got vases, mugs, glasses, and pretty much anything that would hold water. They arranged the flowers, took the loot home, and put flower arrangements all over their houses. They christened it "The Flower Fling," and my life was never the same! Bless their hearts, they taught me to take the brakes off and enjoy the garden with all my might.

The kids were such a joy, I had them come more often, but first we developed some basic ground rules:

- Don't come over without an invitation.
- Always ask your parents' permission.
- Get my okay before you pick something because it might be for a photo.

And the most important:

- There are people places and plant places. The paths are for people and the beds are for plants.

Oh, how indignant they became when a child who was new to the garden stepped in one of my garden beds! Soon I was photographing the kids planting peas, pulling carrots, and harvesting strawberries.

Then we got a little more sophisticated. I was doing a story on squash and decided that children would make the photos more interesting, so I invited a few of my enthusiastic young neighbors for a squash pollinating session. I thought I did a great job of explaining the process of taking pollen from a male squash plant on a Q-Tip and transferring it to a female squash to make a new variety. I started clicking away, got a few photos, and then they decided it would be more interesting if they crossed a squash with a tomato to make a squashy-tomato and a squash with a sunflower to make tall squash, and then they were off "Q-Tipping" all over the garden. So much for my squash photos. Then there was a sunflower planting that morphed into a "let's use Ros's garden hand lens and go look for spiders" session.

A few years into this project it became clear to me that I needed to have garden photos that looked different from season to season and from year to year. Since I'm a landscape designer by profession, changing the garden isn't actually as hard or expensive as it may seem. When my contactor does an installation for me at a client's home, it often involves removing a rotting fence or deck, which includes lumber we can salvage. A delivery of new bricks or slate often includes pieces too thin or uneven to lay, or a few more than are needed. Instead of paying to take them to the dump, the contractor delivers these to my yard. My gardener usually helps redo the garden, but for a big project, such as putting in a maze for an Alice in Wonderland garden (yes, a maze, and we grew cherry tomatoes, snap beans, and mini-pumpkins on it), my contractor chooses an off day between projects and sends his crew over to install it.

I've had a lot of fun choosing different themes for each season. For instance, since 1992 was the five-hundredth anniversary of Columbus landing in the New World, I decided that a garden full

of New World plants would be appropriate—filled with squashes, beans, chilies, tomatoes, amaranths, and sunflowers. Of course, I've had lots of gardens with an edible theme, like a spring garden filled with edible flowers and salad greens, and a spice garden, where I grew out the more obvious herbs whose seeds are spices (fennel, anise, cumin, dill, coriander) plus a large patch of unusual mustards for seed—brown, white, and black—that made some of the freshest condiments I'd ever tasted. I gave away jars of the mustards during the holiday season to much acclaim. Then there was the salsa garden, the Italian wild greens garden, and a rainbow vegetable garden featuring all the colorful vegetables. This year I have a grain garden that was filled with wheat and flax in the spring, and is planted with heat-loving corn and amaranths for the summer.

Some of the most interesting gardens I planned around "my kids." One summer I had them plant pumpkins along the street for a Halloween harvest. That fall I designed a fenced-in secret garden for Sandra, my ten-year-old next-door neighbor. The next spring it was filled to overflowing with potatoes and non-edible sweet peas, followed by popcorn, beans, and cherry tomatoes in summer. For two years I had fairy gardens; the little girls in the neighborhood made fairies from all sorts of materials and partially hid them around the garden. I included plants with fairy names like "The Fairy" rose, "Elfin" thyme, and "Pixie Beauty" daylily.

My niece Nancy Jane suggested I do something "really interesting." "Like what?" I asked. "A Wizard of Oz garden," she said. As I wondered aloud what such a garden would look like, she piped up, "It would have a yellow brick road." The idea was so inspired that practically the whole family as well as lots of friends joined in. My daughter-in-law's mother built the Tin Man from watering cans, plastic plant containers, and dryer vent pipes—all sprayed silver. We had a scarecrow-making party to build the rest of the characters. We dressed Dorothy, the Scarecrow, and the Cowardly Lion in inexpensive clothes from the Goodwill resale shop, and even found a pair of red pumps that the kids covered with glue and sprinkled with red glitter. The denizens of Oz lived in a large stand of corn surrounded with lots of zinnias. Many of the children made it a ritual to walk down the yellow brick road (painted bricks) on their way to school. The next year we recycled the scarecrows and made an American Gothic garden with the characters in front of a false-front Victorian house surrounded with a classic American vegetable garden of beans, corn, squashes, and tomatoes.

Chickens (yes, I have chickens in my suburban front yard!) were the perfect addition to what was in the process of becoming a perfect place for both plants and people. The chickens recycle the garden and kitchen waste, and they give us fabulous fresh eggs, usually one a day per hen, which gives us plenty to share with our neighbors. Of course, roosters are very loud at 5:00 a.m., so Mr. X (our very spoiled, hand-raised rooster) comes into the garage every night and roosts in a dog carrier. This is not a problem, since he comes to the coop door to come in at night and follows us out to the coop in the morning. You see, unlike most chickens, when he hatched Mr. X imprinted on a human—my husband, Robert—not on his chicken mom, so he follows us around like a puppy. The hens, which know that they are chickens, are in their coop 24/7. A few years after getting chickens, I planted a row of French sorrel out by the street and trained the kids to harvest a few leaves at a time and stick them through the chicken wire for Mr. X and the hens. This has been a big attraction; in fact, children from blocks away now drag visiting grandparents and friends over to see the chickens and feed them. Mr. X is now thirteen years old and joined by a new little flock of hens we raised from eggs, and there's a new flock of little children coming by to feed them most days.

From a few vegetables in the front yard to a living paradise—how my life has changed! Every morning I wake up and can't believe my good fortune. This morning I made my usual cup of tea and headed out to see what has changed in my Garden of Eden. Are the strawberries ripe enough to pick for breakfast? What flowers shall I pick for the vase on my desk? And how are my dear chickens? It's June, and it must be almost time for the senior prom. I know because my neighbors just asked if their daughter and her boyfriend could have their portrait taken in my garden. And a toddler across the street called out the front window, "Ros, Ros, chickens." It's going to be another great day!

Edible Estates is an attack on the front lawn and everything it has come to represent!

Edible Estates is an ongoing series of projects that replaces the front lawn with edible garden landscapes responsive to culture, climate, context, and people!

Edible Estates reconciles issues of global food production and urban land use with the modest gesture of a small domestic garden!

Edible Estates is a practical food-producing initiative, a place-responsive landscape design proposal, a scientific horticultural experiment, a conceptual land-art project, a defiant political statement, a community outreach program, and an act of radical gardening!

Edible Estates is nothing new; growing our own food is the first thing we did when we stopped being nomadic and started being "civilized"!

About the Edible Estates Gardens

Edible Estates is an ongoing initiative to create a series of regional prototype gardens that replace domestic front lawns and other unused spaces in front of homes with places for families to grow their own food. The eight gardens planted thus far, which are presented in the following pages, have been established in cities across the United States and in England. Adventurous residents in each town have offered their front lawns as working prototypes for their regions. Each of these highly productive gardens is very different, designed to respond to the unique characteristics of the site, the needs and desires of the owner, the community and its history, and, especially, the local climate and geography.

Most of the gardens are commissioned by local art institutions and developed in partnership with horticultural, agricultural, or community gardening organizations. Working together with the owners, neighbors, friends, and local volunteers, we plant each garden in the spring or early summer. The story of the garden's creation and its first season of growth is presented with a public exhibition, which includes videos, weekly garden portraits by a local photographer, a series of workshops on growing food, and printed brochures featuring local planting calendars and gardening resources.

These simple, low-cost gardens and their stories are meant to inspire others; they demonstrate what is possible for anyone with the will to grow food and some unused land between the house and the street. Unlike the unattainable images of perfection we see in design and gardening magazines, you should be able to look at the Edible Estates gardens presented here and imagine doing something similar, or even better, in front of your own house. These pages contain real-life gardens that are tended by typical families in a variety of common living situations, from homes in the outer suburbs to inner-city apartments.

With the modest gesture of reconsidering the use of our small, individual, private front yards, the Edible Estates project invites us to reconsider our relationships with our neighbors, the sources of our food, and our connections to the natural environment immediately outside our front doors. The following pages present the stories, mostly in the words of the gardeners themselves, of the eight completed gardens.

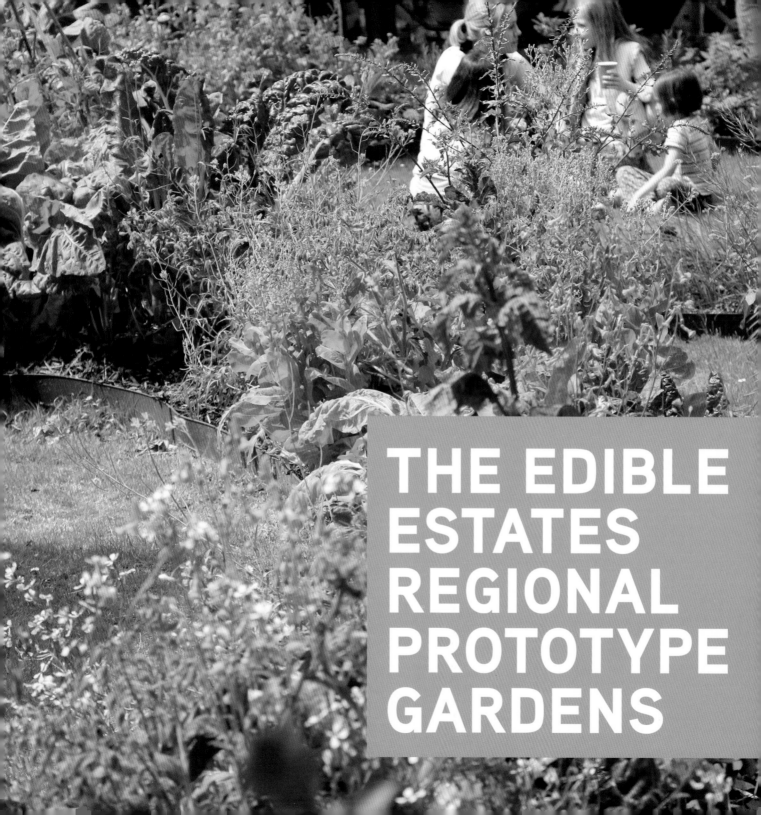

THE EDIBLE ESTATES REGIONAL PROTOTYPE GARDENS

About the Regional Prototype Garden Sites

Prototype garden locations are selected for maximum impact and influence. We want to plant Edible Estates where they are least likely to exist otherwise and where they will provide a vivid contrast with the surrounding landscapes of suburban lawns or inner-city concrete. Each prototype provides local inspiration and momentum to plant gardens in situations not previously considered.

Edible Estates gardens are established on streets where the interruption of the endless lawn is dramatic and controversial. A monotonous housing development of identical homes and front lawns would be ideal! Our dream is to be arrested for planting vegetables in a front lawn in a housing development or town where it is illegal.

The layout, design, and plant list of each garden is developed in collaboration with the family who owns it. The garden is planted with the help of friends, neighbors, and local volunteers, and all costs associated with establishing it for the first season are covered.

We look for prototype garden sites that conform to the following parameters.

The front yard:
* is very visible from the street, with regular car or pedestrian traffic
* has good solar access, ideally with a south or southwest orientation
* is relatively flat, with few large trees or major landscaping that can't easily be removed

The house or apartment building:
* represents a typical or common living situation
* opens on to the front yard with windows or a front door
* provides an iconic domestic backdrop to the Edible Estate garden

The prospective Edible Estate owners:
* are avid and knowledgeable gardeners who are enthusiastic about the project
* are eager to share their stories of front yard gardening
* are committed to continuing the Edible Estate prototype garden indefinitely

Basic Guidelines for Making an Edible Estate

What You May Need:

* stakes and string to lay out a design
* a sod-cutter and a rototiller
* newspapers to cover the lawn for mounded plantings or raised beds
* shovels, hand trowels, and rakes
* compost to amend or cover existing soil
* an irrigation system, such as soaker hoses or drip lines
* fencing material to deter animals
* a composting system (prefabricated bins, wood slats, chicken-wire enclosures, etc.)
* mulch material (bark, straw, wood chips, etc.) to cover several inches of the soil
* seeds, starts, or trees of the vegetables, herbs, and fruits selected for your region
* friends and neighbors to help

Some Questions to Consider:

* How is our **dirt**? Does the soil test tell us that amendments are needed or that there are traces of lawn chemicals?
* Where is **south**? Where are the shady and sunny areas?
* To establish a permanent **structure**, where should tall trees or lower ground cover go? Are there views to frame or obscure?
* What do we want to **eat** from our estate? What do we like that we can't find at the local market?
* It is good to go **vertical** for higher yields and/or in small spaces. Do we have something on which fruits and vegetables on vines can grow?
* How do we want to **move** through our Edible Estate? Where should paths go and where should plants go?
* **Mulch** will retain moisture, block weeds, and decompose into the soil. What kind should we use—straw, bark, wood chips, compost, rocks, or leaves? What is locally available?
* Is there an area in our estate for **people**? Will we include a place where we can relax and enjoy watching our plants and food grow?

The Basic Steps:

1 Do a **soil test** to see what sorts of amendments might be needed or if there are traces of lawn chemicals.

2 Make a **plan** for your Edible Estate, and mark it out with stakes and tape.

3 Use a sod-cutter to **remove the lawn**. Roll it up, give it away, or find a new use for it. If you do not have Bermuda grass or another type of rhizomatic lawn, you may **turn over** the existing turf to keep the topsoil and nitrogen-rich grass in your yard. You also can **cover any lawn** with a series of raised beds or mounded plantings.

4 On existing exposed soil, mix in a generous amount of compost, earthworm castings, manure, mushroom soil, and any combination of soil **amendments** that you may need or have access to.

5 During the first few seasons, experiment with **plants**, trying any edibles that are appropriate for your growing zone and establishing seeds, starts, trees, and vines according to your local planting calendar. You will gradually become aware of what does well on your land and what you like to eat. A diverse garden is a healthy garden.

6 Cover the exposed soil with a thick layer of **mulch**.

7 **Water** the plants thoroughly and install soaker hoses or drip lines as necessary for irrigation.

8 Install **fencing** as needed to deter local animal visitors, such as rabbits and deer, if they become an issue.

9 The garden is just the start. The next step is to set up **compost** bins and a **rainwater** catchment system.

Edible Estates

a gardenlab project

EDITION ONE:

SALINA

KANSAS

SALINA, KANSAS

The first edition of the Edible Estates project was established, symbolically, over the Fourth of July weekend, 2005, in Salina, Kansas, the geographic center of the United States. Local residents Stan and Priti Cox had eagerly offered their typical front lawn as a working prototype for the region.

Stan is a plant geneticist at the Land Institute, a world-renowned research institution founded by Kansas native Wes Jackson in 1976. The organization is working to develop an agricultural system with the ecological stability of the prairie and a grain yield comparable to that from annual crops. Priti is an artist originally from Hyderabad, India. The garden was planted with a wide array of edibles that would survive in the extreme prairie climate, including many herbs and vegetables to be used in Priti's Indian dishes such as okra, green chilies, Swiss chard, curry leaf tree, eggplant, and tomatoes (a staple of Indian cooking).

Estate owners: Stan and Priti Cox
Location: Salina, Kansas
Commissioned by: Salina Art Center
USDA plant hardiness zone: 5
Established: July 2–4, 2005
Front yard exposure: East
Size of front yard: 25 x 34 feet

Design, Materials, and Plants

The design for the garden uses two simple elements to define the spaces, creating environments where people and plants can live together. On the left is a large mound that is rich with fertile compost. In it we planted annual vegetables and herbs that will be able to establish deep roots. Those that need well-draining soil are placed closer to the top, and those that like more moisture are planted farther down. On the right and adjacent to the front drive and entry is a recessed circle for seating, which is mulched with bark. It is surrounded by a border of thyme and deciduous fruit trees; these will eventually enclose the space. The front of the garden was planted with okra during the first season, and it completely concealed the house just six weeks after it was planted. The steep slope has been planted with berries. Grape vines planted against the house will eventually grow up a series of trellises. The entire garden has been mulched with straw, which Stan can collect every year from the Land Institute. It will block weeds, retain moisture, and enrich the soil as it decomposes.

When people, land, and community are as one,
all three members prosper;
when they relate not as members
but as competing interests,
all three are exploited.
By consulting Nature as the source
and measure of that membership,
the Land Institute seeks to develop an agriculture
that will save soil from being lost or poisoned
while promoting a community life at once
prosperous and enduring
  – Mission statement, The Land Institute

CURB APPEAL

Stan Cox

I came in from mowing the lawn one hot May evening in 2005 and turned on the computer. By the time I'd finished reading the first e-mail message, I knew my mowing days would soon be over. The sender, Stacy Switzer, was curating a show on food and eating that fall at the Salina Art Center. In her message Stacy told my wife, Priti, and me that the Art Center had commissioned a West Coast artist, Fritz Haeg, to remove a front lawn and replace it with an all-edible planting. She was looking for willing Salina homeowners.

Without hesitating, Priti and I volunteered our yard. There was little reason not to do it. I'd been raising crops of lawn clippings in Kansas for two decades, with nothing to show for my effort. When Priti and I read Stacy's e-mail and then looked out at the patch of Bermuda grass in front of our house, we knew we'd never even miss it. We had no idea what sort of botanical curiosity might take its place, but the lawn could go.

Not that our lawn was the archetypal green monster. We never watered it, never sprayed it, and almost never fertilized it. I cut it with a manual reel-type mower. (I did that because it was quiet and cheap, and I could use the exercise. But on occasion, a neighbor or passerby would feel pity and offer help: "Hey, I have a lawn mower if you want to borrow it!") Bermuda grass is tough as barbed wire, so our lawn had held the soil through the extremes of Kansas summers, winters, and droughts, while easily fending off weeds—except for dandelions, which it had fought to a stalemate. With such minimal management, it posed little threat to nature. But it wasn't good for much of anything either.

I have no quarrel with grass. As a crop breeder, I have spent my career working with food-producing grasses like wheat, sorghum, and oats. Before European settlement, most of Kansas was covered in prairie, which is predominantly grasses. Over the past sixty-five million years, grasses have coevolved with grazing animals, then with humans, always performing important ecological functions. But neither the shocking-green, nitrogen-gorged carpets of McMansionland nor the scruffy little patch of Bermuda grass that once lay in front of our house has much of anything in common with natural grass-covered landscapes. It's lawns, not grasses, that are the scourge of suburbia.

Salina lies in a wide, fertile valley near the confluence of the Saline and the Smoky Hill rivers. The low hills to the east and west remain largely in native or restored prairie, some of it grazed, while the flatlands surrounding the city are sown to wheat, soybean, and sorghum. (The agriculture land closest to town is being paved over for industry, commerce, and suburbs.) Several years of below-average rainfall reached a crisis in the summer of 2006 with a drought severe enough to trigger strict lawn-watering and car-washing restrictions. The first day of a full ban saw the city's water consumption drop by half! Water has

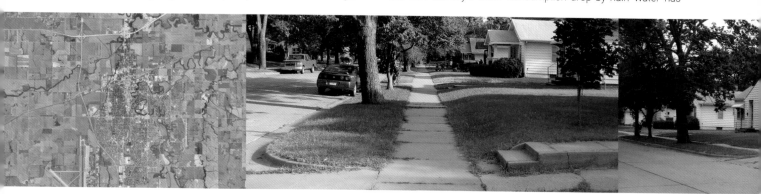

become a very big issue. The main concern is competition for river and groundwater between agriculture and urban/suburban uses. It is exacerbated by a "plume" of industrial contamination that is spreading inexorably toward the city's groundwater source.

Fritz arrived on the Thursday before the July 4th weekend, and by Friday evening, with the help of local volunteers, he'd removed the lawn with a sod-cutter, traded it for partial credit on a truckload of composted manure, tilled the yard, and introduced some topography: a sunken sitting area and a small hill. Saturday we were to plant, and I had some serious doubts about that. Early July is just about the worst time to establish any sort of plantings in Kansas; the seedlings or cuttings that emerge can look forward to two months of heat—often in the triple digits—along with wind and drought, enlivened by the occasional hailstorm. But the Art Center show was scheduled for late September, so it was now or never. We needed a lot of green growth in the next two and a half months, and that meant a lot of fast-growing vegetables and herbs along with transplanted fruit trees, grapes, and berries.

Having come to town empty-handed, Fritz roamed Salina in search of plants and seeds while I gathered other specimens at my workplace. I'm on the staff of the Land Institute, a nonprofit that does research in natural agriculture, so I was able to bring in some wild and semi-wild edible plants and a load of mulch to cover the soil that we'd stripped bare. By Sunday noon, with a lot of help from friends, the Edible Estate was in place. A simple drip system kept everything alive and growing in the weeks that followed, without inflating our water bill too much. Fritz had pulled it off after all. The new front yard looked big and green, indeed lush, in time for its September premiere.

Since that fall we've maintained the trees and perennial herbs but replaced most of the annual plants with deep-rooted, long-lived perennials, to provide year-round ground-cover that takes care of itself; still, one sunny corner remains reserved for annual vegetables. Familiar perennials like strawberries, thyme, blackberries, and horseradish have been joined by plants that the Land Institute is developing as perennial grain crops of the future: intermediate wheatgrass, Maximilian sunflower, and Illinois bundleflower. The plants may be mostly perennial, but the yard is far from static. Unlike an industrial lawn, which is designed to look the same, or nearly the same, year round and year to year, our front yard is in constant flux; hard times for one plant species may be good times for others. The yard is beautiful even when it's brown all winter, as are natural landscapes in Kansas at that time of year. In the growing season, its greenness is intense and never monotonous.

The first question people ask about our Edible Estate is either "Have your neighbors complained?" or "Has the city fined you?" Everyone, it seems, claims to like the new front yard, yet everyone expects others not to like it. Negative neighbor reaction has been the chief preoccupation of most reporters and film crews we've dealt with, including those from the *New York Times* and ABC's *World News Tonight*. When we would assure them that we'd had only positive reactions, they didn't want to believe it. I stood beside one of our neighbors as she told ABC's cameras, "Well, when they started tearing up their yard last year, I thought, 'What the heck's going on over there?' But once they got it done, I liked it." When the report aired, all that viewers heard her say was, "What the heck's going on over there?" Whatever the reality, controversy was the story.

Our new front yard has been welcomed because our neighborhood is not a place where phony "property values" dominate. If we lived in the posh district of east Salina known as The Hill (where there are no houses, only "homes"), we certainly would have faced stiff resistance. Individuals are free to judge the

Salina, Kansas Regional Prototype Garden #1

appearance of front yards based on their own likes and dislikes, but all of that goes out the window when homeowners and the housing industry join forces to defend property values. That has been truer than ever in the twenty-first-century debt economy, in which houses have served as piggy banks. From the curb, an unconventional front yard can easily look much better than a lawn, since a lawn doesn't really look like anything. But that doesn't matter when it comes to property values. It may sound like an aesthetic term, but "curb appeal" is a purely economic concept. When it comes to curb appeal, beauty is in the eye not of the beholder but of the broker.

In a 2003 study of the lawn-chemical industry, Paul Robbins and Julie Sharp, then of Ohio State University, drew a "fundamental lesson of the lawn": that "such self-evident and noncontroversial landscapes are the ones most configured by socioeconomic force relations." Serving as familiar, marketable packaging for "homes," front yards are best kept in a noncontroversial state because standardized commodities are the easiest to mass-market. Robbins and Sharp noted that "property values are clearly associated with high-input green-lawn maintenance and use," and "moreover, lawn-chemical users typically associated moral character and social responsibility with the condition of the lawn." To toss all that aside and grow food in the front yard is an announcement that one has bought a house in order to live in it, not to turn around and sell it at a profit in two years. In the housing economy, such an attitude qualifies as moral laxity.

But front-yard vegetation isn't always a matter of individual choice. Today 57 million Americans—approaching one person out of five—live in homes regulated by homeowner associations. Association members must sign documents called "covenants" that almost always mandate a front lawn and frequently contain provisions like these, sampled from covenants that are being enforced by associations in communities across the country:

- "Lawns shall be watered, fertilized, and sprayed for weeds and/or insects and diseases as needed to keep them healthy and green. They shall be mowed on a regular basis."
- "Sprinklers shall be installed in the front yard of each residence.... [Front yard] shall include, at a minimum, the following: foundation shrubs, three (3) two inch (2") caliper, container-grown trees, ground cover, and grass."
- "Grass shall be maintained at a length not to exceed 4 inches.... Grass shall be maintained at a minimum of a medium green color."
- "Vegetable gardens are to be located between the rear property line and side lines of the house [and] must not exceed 8 feet by 8 feet."

The simplest way to stay out of trouble with the property cops, of course, is to live in a neighborhood that doesn't have private covenants. Our city is like many in having some restrictive subdivisions but a much larger territory that remains free. Our house is in the covenant-free zone. We wake up each morning to the crowing of roosters that belong to neighbors across the alley. (The birds aren't quite legal, but nobody complains.) A couple of streets over, other neighbors have painted the entire front of their house as an American flag. Our Edible Estate, which would probably give the typical homeowner association board member a case of the hives, doesn't bother our neighbors at all.

In much of America, this live-and-let-live attitude is still the rule. Nevertheless, in writing about the lawn question, I've heard from less-fortunate people in states from coast to coast whose unconventional yards have found easy acceptance among their neighbors but have offended the official guardians of property values.

You may have already thought to yourself, "This guy works with plants for a living. A non-lawn like that is going to be a lot more of a hassle if you're a librarian (or trucker or district manager) like me." On that, I can provide some reassurance. Plant breeders, agronomists, and others of our ilk are not avid gardeners or lawn-tenders. After a long, hot summer day in a corn, soybean, or Illinois bundleflower nursery, the last thing a good plant scientist wants to do is go home and toil in the front yard.

Early in my career, before I moved to Salina, a yardwork-averse colleague of mine in agriculture went so far as to promulgate a theory that the amount of energy spent on lawn care by a homeowner is always in inverse proportion to the time spent on sex. We kept that joke running for years (as in, "Say, your yard's looking mighty fine lately, Jim. Everything OK?"). I'm just glad Jim doesn't live in Salina, because our Edible Estate looks as if it takes much more time than it does. No, really; if this new yard were more work than what I've had to do in the past, you can bet I'd have seeded the whole place to a mowable grass at the first opportunity.

So for about the same amount of work as we'd expend on a lawn, we have a front yard that's an identifiable place. In the old lawn, the only geographical feature was a trouble spot in the northeast corner that always turned brown in midsummer. Now every square foot is recognizable, by its elevation, by the plant species growing on it, or both. All around us the neighborhood fleet of mowers, leaf blowers, weed trimmers, and other gas-and-electric-powered contraptions can make a quiet Saturday afternoon sound more like a Monday morning at the sawmill. But aside from digging a dandelion here and there, we can take it easy. The bonus, of course, is that at various times of year we can pick strawberries, chilies, thyme, peaches, grapes, basil, bitter gourds, saskatoons, blackberries, Swiss chard, rhubarb, sage, or other edibles.

Whatever the advantages of alternative yards, the industrial lawn isn't going to just go away. Backed by powerful economic and ideological forces, the lawn culture that we inherited from England has evolved to the point that it's as American as baseball, apple pie, and war. In 2005, when I was working on an article about the lawn racket, I spoke with Den Gardner, executive director of the lawn-and-landscape industry group Project Evergreen. In answer to my very first question, Gardner said he had a story. "And you'll want to use this one, Stan," he said. "I was boarding a flight in Atlanta and a couple of dozen troops with the 101st Airborne, just back from Iraq, got on the plane. They were all fired up about being home. I asked one soldier what three things he'd missed most over there. He listed—in this order—green grass, Domino's pizza, and beer. In that order! I'm telling you, Stan, in this country, with our beautiful lawns and parks, we take 'green' for granted." And you can bet that the companies represented by Project Evergreen can provide a full range of products to create a green that's a couple of shades deeper than anything nature can come up with.

But history hasn't ended after all, and America's circumstances are changing. We may soon find ourselves in an era when houses are valued more for shelter than for speculation, when soil provides more food for people than profit for the petrochemical companies, and when curb appeal isn't enforced by the property cops. So beat the rush, retire your lawnmower, and rent a sod-cutter.

Presented at

Salina Art Center, September 25– December 31, 2005

Thanks to

Becky Atkinson, Pam Harris, Jay Heiman, Wendy Moshier, and Stacy Switzer, Salina Art Center; David Van Tassel, The Land Institute; Katie Bachler and Erin Marshel, for research and assistance; and gardener and volunteer Ted Zerger, Salina

Edible Estates
a gardenlab project

EDITION TWO: LAKEWOOD
CALIFORNIA

LAKEWOOD, CALIFORNIA

From: Michael Foti
Sent: Friday, December 09, 2005 7:44 PM
Subject: Interested in the project

Greetings,
I have just read about your Edible Estates project on the
TreeHugger website and think I might be a good candidate for
you to consider. Our home is about as typical a suburban
mid-fifties tract home as you can get. We're located in the
master of all master-planned communities, Lakewood, CA. Our
lawn is flat, gets plenty of sunlight, and is totally pesticide-
free. It's also one of the brownest on the street, as my wife
refuses to waste water on it.

Dimensions are about 20' x 38', so there's lots of space. We're
semi-experienced, but enthusiastic gardeners. We have an
established vegetable garden in our backyard already.
If you're interested, I can send photos of our house/yard.

Regards,
Michael & Jennifer

Estate owners: Michael, Jennifer,
Cecilia, and June Foti
Location: Lakewood, California
USDA plant hardiness zone: 10
Established: May 27–29, 2006
Front yard exposure: Northeast
Size of front yard: 38 x 20 feet

Design, Materials, and Plants

Over the weekend of the Memorial Day holiday, May 27–29, 2006, we planted the garden with a steady stream of local volunteers, some of them friends and some who heard about the project and just wanted to help out and be part of the process. Here's what we planted in that little 760-square-foot space previously occupied by the lawn:

artichokes
Shishito peppers
Armenian cucumbers
red bell peppers
jalapeño peppers
ivory peppers
cayenne peppers
Gypsy peppers
Purple Beauty
  peppers
chervil
fennel
chamomile
collards

honeydew melons
chives
yellow wax beans
Purple Queen beans
red onions
green bunching
  onions
bush beans
sorrel
Maui onions
Big Max pumpkins
Millionaire eggplants
Habanera peppers
Black Beauty
  eggplants

small sugar pumpkins
Anaheim peppers
English thyme
variegated thyme
French thyme
purple sage
sage
Magic Mountain basil
White Beauty
  eggplants
stevia
Super Sweet
  tomatoes
Champion tomatoes
Momotaro tomatoes

Brandywine tomatoes
chocolate bell
  peppers
Lemon Boy tomatoes
Barbecue rosemary
Greek oregano
Italian oregano
tarragon
creeping thyme
lemon balm
curled parsley
variegated oregano
dwarf curry
lemon cucumbers

Japanese cucumbers
patty pan cucumbers
Bush Champion
  cucumbers
Crimson Sweet
  watermelons
raspberries
boysenberries
pluots
grapes
Santa Rosa plums
figs
Asian pears
Panamint nectarines
Katy apricots

Flavor Delight
  apricots
Snow Queen
  nectarines
Mexican Pear guavas
golden apples
July Elberta peaches
kumquats
pink lemons
Golden Nugget
  mandarins
Washington navel
  oranges
Chandler pomelos
grapefruits

The cities will be part of the country; I shall live 30 miles from my office in one direction, under a pine tree; my secretary will live 30 miles away from it too, in the other direction, under another pine tree. We shall both have our own car. We shall use up tires, wear out road surfaces and gears, consume oil and gasoline. All of which will necessitate a great deal of work... enough for all.

—Le Corbusier, *The Radiant City* (1935)

LOS ANGELES

Since it was settled by native humans thousands of years ago, the Los Angeles region has always been a hospitable area to the production of food. It was once home to the largest concentration of wine vineyards in the country and the capital of citrus production until the population boom and subsequent water wars of the 1920s. Land use was still more than 20 percent agricultural in 1969. While the population of Los Angeles County rose almost 50 percent in the 1950s, the county sacrificed three thousand acres of farmland a day.

Today urban agriculture remains only as an occasional novelty or (in the case of the South Central Farm, which in 2006 was bulldozed to make way for warehouses) an inconvenience whose value is unrecognized by the march of urban "progress." This city was once a combination of fertile flood plain and low chaparral; now 90 percent of it is covered with pavement or buildings. Lawns carpet more than 1.6 million acres in California, and the emissions produced by lawnmowers contribute significantly to its poor air quality.

A few other factors make Los Angeles a perfect place in which to introduce an Edible Estate. The lawn is an easy target in a region that receives no rain for most of the year. The semi-public front lawn in particular is ripe for reconsideration in a city with an extreme introverted focus on the private house as defensible space, and a corresponding lack of accessible public green space.

Los Angeles is the creator, capital, and iconic face of sprawl. The American dream of every house presented on the ornamental carpet of manicured green lawn was brought to the West Coast in the 1950s with the iconic housing development of Lakewood, home to this Edible Estates regional prototype garden. The city of Lakewood comprised one of the first large suburban housing developments in the United States, built concurrently with Levittown, New York. Lakewood lies south of Los Angeles and was constructed on former agricultural land. Here the Lakewood Park Company introduced assembly-line housing developments to California, constructing 17,500 homes on 3,500 acres in little over a year at the rate of about two thousand homes per month. In the last three months of 1950, twenty-five families moved to Lakewood per day.

After six months of searching for just the right house and family for the Los Angeles edition of Edible Estates, the Foti family in Lakewood was selected for the project. Michael and Jennifer did have some concerns about what their neighbors would think. They wanted to make sure that the new garden was a gracious and welcoming gesture. During the previous few years the Fotis had established a modest but serious vegetable garden and chicken coop in the backyard. The entire Foti family, including daughters Cecilia (then age thirteen) and June (then age six), was excited about the prospect of ripping out the lawn to create a space in which to grow their own food.

MICHAEL'S BLOG

Excerpts from Michael Foti's garden blog, a firsthand account of the struggles and rewards of his Edible Estate. "Foti Farm," http://home.roadrunner.com/~fotifamily

Friday, May 26, 2006, 9:24 PM
Taking it to the street (or at least the sidewalk)

We're about to dramatically increase the size of our gardening efforts here on the Foti Farm. As hinted at previously, we are collaborating with architect/non-artist/radical gardener, Fritz Haeg, on a new vegetable garden for the front of the house. Yes, that's right, we're going shock the neighbors, and dig up the lawn! It's the latest installment of Fritz's Edible Estates project¶ Why are we doing this? The honest answer is that it just sounded like fun. I've been aware of Fritz's work ever since I visited an exhibit he did in Pasadena a few years ago called the gardenLAb Experiment. Early this year, I read on the Internet that he was looking for a site here in the Los Angeles area to do this Edible Estates project, so I mentioned it to Jenny, and she said, "go for it." I sent off an e-mail and then we didn't hear anything more. A few weeks later Fritz wrote back, asking for some photos of the lawn. So, I sent those off, and again, we didn't hear anything for several months. Just a few weeks ago, Fritz again contacted us, and this time he seemed ready to go. I'm not sure how many other sites he evaluated (maybe we were the only ones brave/foolish enough to go for it), but when we met him for the first time, he asked if we would like to be the site. We said yes, sent Fritz on his way, then I began to immediately fret about the decision. Will we have enough plants? Will we get enough sun? Where will the water come from? I have no water spigot near the front lawn. What will the neighborhood think? This is supposed to be fun, right? I keep telling myself that.¶ I'm not exactly sure what Fritz's motivations or goals for this project are. Despite the sometimes confrontational statements on his website like, "attack on the American front lawn" or "endless suburban carpet of conformity," I do believe he has good intentions. I would not be participating if I thought otherwise. In one of our first conversations together, I told him that I wasn't interested in alienating people who choose to have lawns. For me, the message cannot be that lawns are bad, and if you have one, you're bad too. I think lawns are valid. I do think that there are other possibilities though. I don't think that thought has occurred to many people. Some people even believe that the option doesn't exist. In some places homeowner association fascism actually does prevent it. I don't want to live in that kind of world.¶ Another misconception about this project that I would like to avoid is the idea that we are attempting a rigorous exercise in sustainable permaculture. That would be great, but to be honest, I don't have the experience to pull it off at this point. I intend to experiment though. Perhaps in a few years we'll be able to call our garden "sustainable." Hopefully civilization won't collapse before I'm ready.¶ This is an exercise in thinking differently about that big flat space in front of our house. Is there any value in that? We'll see. Why is the lawn so ubiquitous? Is there something about modern life that precludes other options? Are our lives too busy? Are our communities so degraded that we must strip our most public of private spaces down to the bare minimum? I think many people view that space between their front door and the street as a kind of Demilitarized Zone. I confess to being worried that somebody will come along and steal "my" vegetables when 'm not looking. What a horrible thought.¶ We're a pretty average family, in a pretty average neighborhood. If we can make it work, anybody can. If we can't, then this project will help identify what I would say are real flaws in our society. I think everybody should be able to grow at least some of their own food. Everybody should be able to create something of beauty in full view of the world. I want to see a more humane interface between public and private space. I want to engage the world, not turn inward. ¶ We begin planting tomorrow, and at this point, I'm excited, and basically over fretting about this project. The unknowns will work themselves out in due course.

Saturday, May 27, 2006, 7:35 PM
Edible Estates Day 1

I have a saying that I like to trot out in situations like this. All adventures have adversity. Usually when I say this, Jenny replies that she doesn't want any more adventures. Today was certainly an adventure, and not one any of us would like to repeat, at least not until tomorrow anyway. ¶ I awoke at dawn to begin excavating the buried sprinkler heads in the lawn so we could avoid them later when using the sod-cutter. A film crew from TreeHugger TV arrived at 11:30, and soon enough I was giving a tour of the grounds and an interview. While this was going on Fritz arrived, and a photographer from the *New York Times* showed up to take pictures of the family and the day's activities. The official project photographer, Taidgh, also showed up about this time and for a while it was a regular media circus around here. That doesn't happen every day. ¶ Things were about to take a dramatic turn for the worse. A delivery truck from the place Fritz had rented a rototiller and sod-cutter from pulled up and dropped off the equipment. Fritz got set up to begin cutting the sod. All the photographers got set to take pictures of the action. Fritz pulled the cord to start the motor. He then pushed the lever to engage the cutting mechanism. The whole rumbling machine came to an abrupt halt. Jenny swears she heard something snap. The whole process was repeated over and over for about an hour while the camera crews looked on. Fritz kept his cool, but I'm sure this was not how he planned for this to go. Eventually it was decided that this sod-cutter was broken beyond any hope. This was a problem because our schedule demands that we get the lawn removed today. By this time, the rental shop had closed for the weekend. We needed a replacement and quick. I got on the phone and found one available at the local Home Depot, but now the problem was that we didn't have a truck to transport it. Home Depot didn't have one to rent either. Fritz left to go figure this all out, while I tried to make the best of the situation by starting to dig up the perimeter of the lawn with a shovel. All the while, the various camera crews sat out on the curb and waited. They were a very nice group of people and we're grateful that they found our project interesting enough to spend their Saturday afternoon at our house. I only wish we could have made it more worth their time. They're all supposed to be back on Monday, when hopefully we'll have a garden for them to shoot. ¶ But first, we still needed to get rid of the lawn. After about an hour Fritz pulled up with a rented U-Haul truck and a rented sod-cutter from Home Depot. We unloaded it (no small trick—they are very heavy) and got ready to go. This time we had success. Finally! Fritz cut one long strip down the length of the lawn, then turned the machine around to head back. Just then, the throttle cable snapped. Ugh! Dead in our tracks again. We fiddled with it a bit and managed to find a way to force the throttle full open. After much effort we got all the sod cut and piled into a mountain on our driveway. Oh yeah, did I mention that the guy who was supposed to haul it all away decided he didn't want it after all? Yep, we now have to figure out another plan to get rid of it. All, I don't know, maybe 3 tons of it. In the meantime, it sits on our driveway. I think I spotted mountain goats perched high atop its lofty peaks. ¶ With the sod removed,

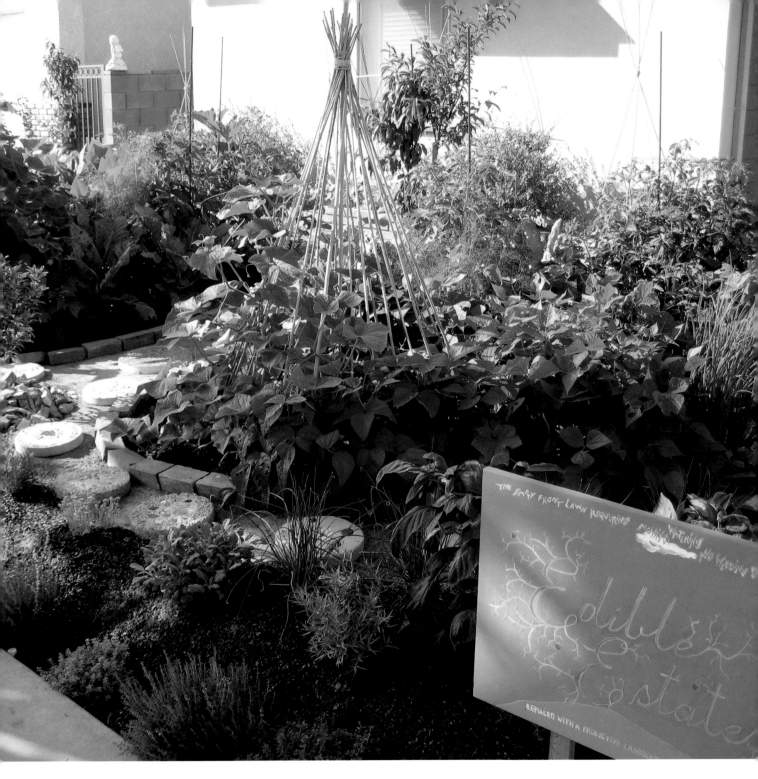

Within the image, the sign reads:

THE EARLY FRONT LAWN REQUIRING ... WATERING ... NO WEEDING ...

Edible Estate

REPLACED WITH A PRODUCTIVE LANDSC...

and the sun rapidly sinking below the horizon, it was now time to rototill the—what do I call it now?—former site of the lawn. This machine was from the same place that rented us the first broken sod-cutter. Turns out they gave us a broken rototiller, too. It was now after 6:00 p.m., and everyone was exhausted. We decided to call it a day. We'll start back up very early tomorrow morning. Fritz hopes to be here by 7:00 a.m. ¶ I forgot to mention the one bright spot of the day. A volunteer named Daniel arrived at about 4:00 to help out with the project. Daniel is a super cool guy who is very interested in the project. He's a recent college graduate who grew up here in Lakewood. He tells us that he's got a small piece of land on the Big Island of Hawaii, and he plans one day to set up a small farm and retreat there. Sounds like a great thing to do to me. We cannot thank Daniel enough for showing up to help. I hope we get to meet him again sometime. ¶ I estimate that we are about half a day behind schedule. That's not horrible, but it's not ideal either. Jenny and the kids really put in a great effort today. I'm so grateful that they support this project, and don't think their dad/husband has gone off the deep end (they aren't saying so to my face anyway). I don't know why I didn't expect there to be setbacks. There are always setbacks. I should have thought back to all the effort it took to build the garden in the backyard. ¶ This isn't easy. I'm sure that we will succeed though, and the eventual victory will be all the sweeter.

Monday, May 29, 2006, 6:13 AM
Day 2

It's kind of hard to believe how much progress was made today. The garden is essentially planted. There are some details to take care of tomorrow, but the bulk of the job is now behind us. Lots of great volunteers showed up today and that really helped to get it all done. Up to this point, it's been very hard to imagine what the garden would actually look like in front of our house. Now that it's here, I'm generally pleased with the results.

Tuesday, May 30, 2006, 6:47 AM
Day 3

Today was considerably less intense than the past two days. We put in soaker hoses in the main planting areas, mulched everything, and placed some rocks around the bases of the trees. We also filled the central, hmmm... we need a new word here, how 'bout, "gardening platforms," with gravel. These are the circular areas at the center of the two vegetable beds where the gardener can position himself to weed, seed and feed all the plants surrounding him. I'm thinking maybe I also need to get up at sunrise each morning and sing to the plants from these spots as well. ¶ It would be wrong to say that we are done. As I said yesterday, this weekend is really just the birth of the garden. Now it must grow and, hopefully, thrive. ¶ I'm glad all the hard work is behind us now. The amount of work accomplished in just three days made for a very draining experience. I'm now hoping to settle into a more relaxing routine with the garden. I think, at least for the next few months, I will get up at about 6:00 in the morning and spend about an hour out there doing whatever needs to be done, watering, weeding, etc. This is a high-maintenance garden. I plan to deal with that by doing small amounts of work on a very consistent basis. I think this is better than doing lots at one time. A lot of that hour a day is just going to be looking around at the garden and enjoying it. I think it's very important to just observe the garden and see what is going on. So often things are happening at a small scale, and you really have to slow down and watch closely to notice. It's hard to really explain how important this is. Gardeners know what I mean.

Thursday, June 01, 2006, 10:12 PM
First impressions

So, it's been a few days now and it still feels like there has been a disturbance in the force. We never really paid much attention to the front of the house when the lawn was there. The way this house is built, you can't even see the front lawn except from the kitchen window. Now, the space exerts a psychic energy that, I must admit, I'm still getting used to. I went out the other morning and just sat on the brick planter along the garage wall for a while. It was quiet and cool out, and this was the first time I've been able to relax and just take it all in. I think it has great potential, but it's a bit raw right now. It feels a bit weird to spend time out there in front of the whole neighborhood. I feel like I'm on display.¶ The neighborhood has been watching. We've noticed quite a few people taking the time to walk by, especially in the mornings and evenings. One older couple has passed by in their car on several occasions. They finally worked up the courage to walk by and I don't think they approved. Jenny heard the woman tsk and shake her head in disgust. This has been the only negative reaction we're aware of. Most people seem to really like it. Jenny saw someone stop and take one of the brochures from the box on the Edible Estates sign. ¶ The plants are doing ok. It's been really hot the last few days. Certainly some of the hottest days of the year so far. The first day, the plants looked kind of crispy, but I gave everything a good, deep watering, which they hadn't had up to that point, and now they look a little better. I think in a week or so the initial shock of transplantation will wear off, and we should have a good idea of what's going to make it or not.

Saturday, June 03, 2006, 3:18 PM
Hot, hot, hot

It's currently 92 degrees out. Hottest day of the year so far. The poor plants are baking in the newly planted garden. I watered everything as best as I could this morning, but in this kind of heat these young plants are having a very rough time. We're going to lose some for sure. Ideally we would have planted about a month ago, instead of a week ago. That would have given them a better chance to get established and be in better shape to survive the heat of summer.

Sunday, June 04, 2006, 9:30 PM
Omens. Good or bad?

Late Sunday evening on the day we first planted the garden, everyone had left, except Fritz, Jenny, and me. The sun was starting to go down and we were kind of admiring our hard work for the first time. A large black bird swooped overhead in a graceful arc, then landed on the very tip of one of the bamboo trellises. The bird sat there for a moment and checked out the new garden. I got the feeling it approved of the change.

Thursday, June 08, 2006, 8:33 AM

We had some light rain this morning, so I skipped the usual morning watering routine. I'm sure it did the plants some good. The overcast skies and cooler temperatures are a lot easier on the plants than the wilting heat wave of the past weekend.¶ I'm beginning to see the first signs of the lawn attempting to fight back. I'm plucking little green shoots of grass whenever I come across them. It's only a few here and there at this point. In the tilled plant beds the soil gives easily, but in the compacted paths it's very hard to rip these "weeds" out. The shoots usually break off at the base before I can get the root out.

Sunday, June 18, 2006, 10:45 AM

Scenes from the garden

The first tomato of the season arrived! We were able to whip up the season's first batch of salsa with homegrown tomatoes and peppers yesterday. Mmm...Can't wait to put this on some huevos rancheros made with eggs from our backyard chickens. These are the rewards of all the hard work for the past few weeks.¶ The front-yard melon/squash patch is really starting to take over. I spent some time this morning thinning out the vines, leaving the best established ones. Lots of these already have melons on them. I really hope I can get these to maturity without having them split open like the watermelons I grew last summer. As they get bigger, I need to watch the water intake.

Monday, June 19, 2006, 3:22 PM

What's it to you?

The *Los Angeles Times* ran a short blurb on the Edible Estates project last week. They printed our address, so I wasn't surprised when I noticed a few strange cars driving by the house this weekend. They'd pull up in front of the house and go real slow, peering out the windows at the garden. A few actually got out to take a look. I greeted a few of these folks and spoke to them a bit about the garden and the project in general. Some expressed surprise that the *Times* would print the address of a private residence. More than one commented that they would be afraid that someone would come along and steal their vegetables if they tried something like our garden in their own yard. Of course I had the same concerns at first, and I've had this discussion with other people who've stopped by to see the garden in the past. It's really interesting how often this comes up. Kind of sad, really.¶ I guess that in person, one of the things that is most striking about the garden when you first see it is how open and close to the sidewalk it is. How vulnerable it seems. There's no fences or anything to keep anybody out. It really makes you aware of how most lawns function as kind of buffer between public and private space. In a way, it sort of illuminates the value of a lawn to most people—not worth stealing, and useful only to the extent that it keeps people away, or doesn't need to be worried about.¶ Many people don't even take any pride in maintaining their own lawn. They pay a service to do it, usually when they aren't around to see (or hear) it being done. One of the concerns I've heard from some neighbors is that they fear I might have taken on more than I can handle in terms of maintenance. Lawns are so easy to deal with, especially if somebody else is doing the work. There is nothing low-maintenance about our garden, and you really can't pay someone to give it the kind of care it needs. I couldn't afford it anyway. If I slack off on the maintenance, it will turn into an eyesore very quickly. I think that is a valid concern, but do people really prefer their neighborhoods be maintained by low-paid workers whose main concern is efficiency rather than beauty? I think it's a vicious cycle. The more utilitarian and functional these spaces become, the easier they are to maintain, but also the easier they are to ignore and neglect. Ultimately, the upkeep of a lawn becomes nothing more than a kind of tax on the homeowner that he only pays out of some sense of obligation, or self-interest in neighborhood property values.

Thursday, June 22, 2006, 8:57 PM

Revenge

I went out into the garden the other morning and discovered that some of my plants were being eaten by caterpillars. I picked 'em all off and fed them to the chickens.

Wednesday, June 28, 2006, 11:23 PM
It is called EDIBLE Estates after all
We're starting to get a lot of produce from the gardens. Last night Jenny prepared a delicious meal of Indian food, made largely from our homegrown vegetables. She used our eggplant, zucchini, onion, garlic, peppers, cilantro, and beans. With the exception of the rice, lentils, spices, and the chicken, this was nearly an entirely homegrown meal. If we were willing to butcher one of our chickens (we aren't), we could have provided that as well. Jenny is a fantastic chef, and we're so lucky to be able to enjoy the meals she prepares. That we grew so much of it ourselves just makes it that much sweeter.

Sunday, July 02, 2006, 10:09 AM
The Good Life
We're enjoying a pretty nice weekend, here on the farm. I'm harvesting lots of fresh veggies in the morning, and in the afternoon we're keeping busy preparing lots o' tasty dishes with those veggies, including a summer classic of tomato, basil, and mozzarella salad.

Saturday, July 15, 2006, 4:09 PM
Gratitude
Currently, the thermometer reads 96 degrees outside. We've started harvesting beans in great numbers today. Really pretty Purple Queen beans. So far we've collected two big bowls full, and the plants still have a lot more on them. A reporter from the *Whole Life Times* stopped by this morning when Jenny and I were picking the beans to interview us for a story, and to take some pictures of the garden. One of the things I mentioned to her was that vegetable gardening, even on a small scale, really helps you appreciate the efforts of the people we depend on to grow our food, the farmers. Jenny, who at this point had been bent over picking beans for about twenty minutes in the hot sun, made a much better observation: picking beans for twenty minutes gives you a greater appreciation for the backbreaking labor done by migrant field workers.

Wednesday, July 19, 2006, 4:17 PM
Vanity
Like a lot of people, when I first started gardening I spent a lot of time looking at photos of beautiful, perfect gardens in glossy gardening magazines. I'd turn the pages of the garden-porn and fantasize about how my garden would one day be just as flawless and stunning. Of course, the realist in me knew that I'd probably fall short. There would be weeds and insect-eaten leaves. Desiccated plants would be found next to others practically drowning in too much water. I'd love the garden, like a parent loves a homely child, but I couldn't realistically expect to ever see images of it printed in the *New York Times* garden pages. Funny how things turn out, huh?¶ I fully realize the *Times* was interested in our garden for the (overblown) controversy surrounding its placement, rather than its beauty, or my stellar gardening skills. Still, they did print pictures of it, and while I think they turned out pretty well, those pictures are sort of the equivalent of a Sears family portrait, where Mom has made sure the kids all have their hair combed, and Dad is wearing the only tie he owns that doesn't have a big stain on the front of it, and everybody has been told to smile. In other words, those pictures lie. Our garden has insect-eaten leaves and brown, dried-out plants. A few weeks ago, when those pictures were taken, the garden was at its youthful visual peak. Today, well, she's starting to look just a little long in the tooth.¶ The "problem" with being published in the *Times* is that lots of people take notice

and want to come by and see the garden. Some of these people want to take pictures and publish them as well. This prospect momentarily sent me into a fit of weeding and pruning, but I've resorted to being philosophical about it. Gardens are living things that get pimples and have awkward growth spurts. They age and get wrinkles. The garden doesn't care how it looks though. Only the gardener does (and maybe the neighbors).

Tuesday, August 01, 2006, 10:54 PM
Reaping what you sow
Without a doubt, the very best thing to come out of our participation in the Edible Estates project has been the opportunity to meet so many nice people. From all the volunteers who came to help plant the garden, to neighbors from the surrounding community, to the folks who read about the project in the paper and then made the trip out to see the garden in person, we've had a steady stream of visitors for the last two months. Some of these people just give a wave and a thumbs-up from their car window as they drive by. Others will stop and tell stories about their own gardens, or offer advice and encouragement. We've tried not to let anybody leave without taking some of our harvest with them, even if it's just a few tomatoes. It's very gratifying to think about how many people are getting to enjoy "our" vegetables. It's kind of amazing to me how many people this garden has touched, even if only in a small way. People I haven't seen or spoken to in years have either read about the project in the paper, or saw the TV news report, and have contacted us to let us know that they got a kick out of it.

Tuesday, August 22, 2006, 4:40 PM
Lakewood
I live here because Lakewood is adequate to the demands of my desire, although I know there's a price to pay. A Puritan strain in American culture is repelled by desires like mine, and has been since a brilliant young photographer named William A. Garnett, working for the Lakewood Park corporation, took a series of aerial photographs in 1950 that look down on the vulnerable wood frames of the houses the company was putting up at the rate of five hundred a week. Even after fifty years, those beautiful and terrible photographs are used to indict suburbia. Except you can't see the intersection of character and place from an altitude of five hundred feet, and Garnett never came back to experience everyday life on the ground. – From *An Ordinary Place*, by author D. J. Waldie, perhaps Lakewood's best-known resident. This greater truth about everyday life on the ground, for me, is exactly what this project is all about. ¶ I myself am sometimes given to bouts of pessimism. When I look around our neighborhood today, I often wonder if Lakewood can remain, in Waldie's words, adequate to the demands of our desires. I shake my head in regret every time I see another modest Lakewood home converted into a edge-to-edge lot-filling McMansion. Nobody ever complains about the effect on community property values when one of those out of scale monsters pops up next door. That's progress, they say. I look at the proliferation of ever bigger RV's and boats in my neighbors' driveways and I wonder how they manage to afford it all. Are they putting it all on credit, living for today like there's no tomorrow, because in their hearts they fear there might not be? ¶ There are other occasions though when I'm reminded of all the other reasons people live here that have nothing to do with satisfying consumerist desires. The house next door to ours has sat empty and vacant for most of this year. Earlier this summer, when we began the Edible Estates project, the house was put up for sale and we wondered if the presence of our front-yard garden would scare people away from moving in next to us. Months went

by and the lawn grew unkempt, shaggy and brown from lack of water and regular maintenance. Then just a few weeks ago, a moving van pulled up and a family with two small boys jumped out. My younger daughter, June, quickly made friends. It wasn't long before June was leading the two-year-old boy around the garden helping him pick (and eat) cherry tomatoes. From the look of wonder in his eyes, I'm fairly certain this was the first time the child had ever seen real food being grown.

Monday, August 28, 2006, 7:10 AM
Out with the old, in with the new

I spent this weekend pulling up old plants and putting in some new ones. It's a difficult time. Too hot for cool-weather crops, but too late in the season for warm-weather ones. I'm splitting the difference. I've put in some cucumbers and squash, which, being warm-weather crops, might do ok, or they might do nothing. As for cool-weather crops, I've put in various lettuces, carrots, bok choy, radicchio, and onions. Over the next month I'll probably put in a lot of other cool-weather plants.

Monday, September 18, 2006, 9:39 AM
Garden update

You can tell the days are getting shorter now. In a few weeks, the weekend will be the only time I'll be able to work in the garden in the daylight. We are getting some food from our odd mix of warm-weather/cool-weather plants these days. Okra is producing very well right now. We gave some to our new neighbors yesterday, after one of their boys said they eat it. We're still getting some tomatoes, although the end is near. The lettuces I planted a few weeks ago are big enough to take cuttings from, so we're enjoying green leafy salads. I pulled up all the eggplant yesterday and replaced it with broccoli. Broccoli has such a pretty blue-green leaf. Hopefully I can keep the caterpillars from eating them this time. We planted a few more cucumbers a few weeks ago, and they actually are starting to get cucumbers on them, so the gamble might pay off. I started a bunch of seeds a couple of weeks ago, but nothing has sprouted up yet. I'm starting to think I planted them too deep. If nothing comes up by next weekend, I'll have to try again.

FRONT YARD OR BARNYARD?
Cecilia Foti, 7th grade

Was the Garden of Eden grass? No. It was a natural wonder of flora and fauna through and through. The American lawn needs to be eradicated from our society and fast! To begin with, lawns endanger our water source and environment. Second, there are some more productive alternatives, such as vegetable gardens, which add variety to our homes. Finally, adding a vegetable or fruit garden provides some surprising health benefits.

Removing the lawns in America will help save our environment and possibly lives. "Seventeen of the thirty commonly used pesticides were found in groundwater and twenty-three have the potential to enter it," says Fritz Haeg. This is very true for California. Water is wasted from pesticides contaminating the groundwater and from overwatering, especially during the hottest times of the day, when water evaporates quickly. Pesticides also run off into the oceans, kill bugs that protect our plants, and hurt animals. Mowers and lawn edgers pollute our air with greenhouse gasses. Many people are concerned with the environment's care and by removing our lawns and not using pesticides, we can help ensure the environment's safety.

Now that the lawn is gone, what to do with that space? Plant a vegetable garden! There are some better, more productive alternatives to lawns, which add variety and texture to your yard and can be visually appealing as well. Many fruits and vegetables come in a variety of colors and can be arranged in the style you choose. You can choose plants in colors that coordinate with your house. Lettuces and tomatoes come in a wide range of colors and patterns from yellow to red to green to purple! Chilies and peppers also come in many colors too. Fruit trees add texture and shade to your home. The produce you grow can be used for cooking or decoration and can even reduce grocery costs. Everyone can find a plant to fit his or her lifestyle.

There is no doubt about it that fruits and vegetables have amazing health benefits. Fruits and vegetables contain many vitamins and minerals, such as vitamin A. These nutrients are necessary to proper bodily functions. For example, spinach provides iron, which is good for the blood. Potatoes and beans contain fiber and tomatoes have lycopene, which is good for the eyes and heart and is a natural antioxidant. Vitamin C, found in oranges, is good for your eyes and skin. Eating vegetables keeps people healthy and can be eaten in many ways to make eating them fun.

Some Americans say lawns are no harm. Some experts even say that pesticide use in California has reduced in previous years. Sulfur use is down by 46,000 pounds. Chemical levels in water are depreciating at a steady rate. Some homeowners might not have time to care for a garden. Many people also take pride in their lawns and care for them. Some homeowners are concerned that property values will drop due to the unusualness of a vegetable garden in their front yard. But even with all these facts, there are still some major problems and health risks.

Although contaminated water percentages are down, there are still some major environmental and health problems with lawns. California has one of the highest uses of pesticides in all 50 states. Even though sulfur use is down, the decrease is only by 1%. Seventeen chemicals, including some very toxic ones, have been traced in the California water source, some of which can harm people. People with lawns and pests could use organic pesticides or homemade remedies. You could use a push mower instead of a gas mower. I ask you, do you want to pollute the earth?

Lawns in America should be removed. By adding a vegetable garden, you can get some amazing health benefits and add variety to your home, while not endangering the environment. I don't know anyone who would not want to improve upon his or her health and save the environment. So try adding a few vegetables to your yard today. Who knows, you may end up planting an entire garden.

"DON'T MOW THIS 'LAWN': FAMILY REPLACES LAKEWOOD LAWN WITH FRUIT, VEGETABLES"

Editorial, Lakewood *Press-Telegram*, July 17, 2006

We tend to think we do all of the teaching when it comes to children. Then they do something poetic, and we realize that we are more often students of their subtle wisdom.

Take Lakewood youngster Cecilia Foti, who wrote an essay at Bancroft Middle School addressing the controversy over her family's decision to convert its front yard into a fruit-and-vegetable farm.

Cecilia, who was profiled in a *New York Times* story also published in the *Press-Telegram*, argued that the old-fashioned front lawn "needs to be eradicated from our society and fast!"

We don't entirely agree with that absolutist view, but we are encouraged by her willingness to write down her thoughts and turn them in at school. We also like the idea of healthy greens sprouting in the place of thirsty grass. Getting kids to talk about vegetables, much less eat them, is a weedy issue. Maybe if more kids grew greens they would eat them.

But more importantly we believe it's OK for the Fotis to do what they want with their yard as long as they don't destroy the character of the neighborhood. And, after examining photos of the yet-to-mature garden, we think the suburban farm fits.

Because of the home's ample driveway, the vegetable patch is rather small and less intrusive than one might think. Planted Memorial Day weekend, the plants are still immature. These aren't the cornstalks you saw in "Field of Dreams."

We're not sure if we'd follow their lead, but we admire the family's decision to turn the lawn into a food source that puts water to a logical use, growing food, rather than a decorative use, greening grass.

Lakewood is known for a live-and-let-live ethos, where residents tend to believe, rightly, that they can do what they want with their land as long as the use doesn't hurt the quality of life for their neighbors. Fruits and veggies can certainly do no more harm to a neighborhood's appearance than the mammoth motor homes legally parked citywide.

We admire Cecilia's commitment to healthy eating, something not nearly enough middle schoolers embrace. Cecilia is now a champion of the garden's edibles. We wish more kids would follow her lead.

Stuck in her vegetable patch is this message: "The empty front lawn requiring mowing, watering and weeding previously on this location has been removed."

Some neighbors, of course, are on the other side of the Fotis' decision to raze their lawn as part of a greater nationwide movement to replace lawns with gardens. Detractors don't think it fits in with the post-war tract homes dotting the city, and we agree it takes some getting used to.

The New York Times described their discontent far more elegantly than we can: "Neighbors fret about a potential decline in property values, while others worry that all those succulent fruits and vegetables will attract drive-by thieves—as well as opossums and other vermin—in pursuit of Maui onions and Brandywine tomatoes."

We cannot believe this small garden will hurt property values, which tend to be dictated by good schools and safe streets, two things Lakewood has going for it. And Lakewood, known for watchful neighbors, needn't worry much about vegetable theft.

Still, we can understand that residents don't necessarily want to look at something they're not used to seeing. But in a nation of unhealthy people, and in a state prone to drought, the Fotis put their front yard to good use. Maybe some will follow.

Critics should tend to their own gardens.

Presented at

Millard Sheets Gallery, Pomona, September 8– October 1, 2006, as part of the exhibition *Fair Exchange*, and at Machine Project, Los Angeles, October 5–29, 2006

Plants and materials donated by

Armstrong Garden Centers

Photography by

Taidgh O'Neill

Thanks to

Volunteer garden workers Katie Bachler, Preston Brown, Winston Kahn, Mitchell Kane, Melissa McDonnell, Taidgh O'Neill, Daniel Procter, Stephanie Scott, Roopa Shenoy, and Aubrey White; Mark Allen, Machine Project; Dan Danzig, Millard Sheets Gallery; Irene Tsatsos; Durfee Foundation; and Katie Bachler and Aubrey White, for research and assistance

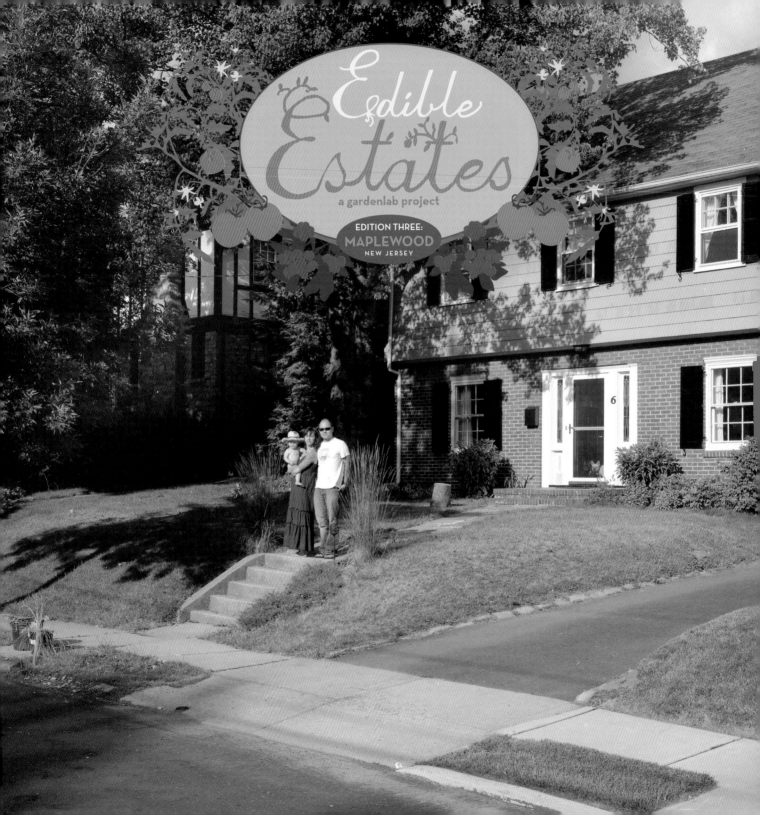

Edible Estates

a gardenlab project

EDITION THREE:
MAPLEWOOD
NEW JERSEY

MAPLEWOOD, NEW JERSEY

From: Michelle Christman
Sent: Monday, June 04, 2007 1:54 PM
Subject: new york city garden to convert? take my lawn, please!

we bought our house in maplewood, new jersey, 2 years ago. maplewood is a small, well manicured, 1920s charmer of a town with a super-progressive community just 27 minutes by train from penn station in new york city. it is a classic town with classic lawns. my husband chris wei (a composer and retired chef), my 1-year-old son atticus huckleberry wei, and our two french bulldogs (bodhi and yoda) have been trying to get more green everyday. i stumbled on your site and see that you were still looking for a home for this year. we'd love it if you're interested in us! our front lawn faces south/southwest. all the other lawns on our block (and quite frankly, in our town) are well groomed. they are also largely uninterrupted as front lawns can't have fences in our town due to local ordinances. in fact, on mondays on our block, it becomes nearly impossible to work (and nearly impossible for my son to nap) because the lawn guys go from yard to yard with their big industrial mowers and blowers and weed-whackers!

we are super enthusiastic about the project and committed and willing to continue the Edible Estates prototype as long as we live in the house.

Estate owners: Michelle Christman, Chris Wei, and Atticus Huckleberry Wei
Location: Maplewood, New Jersey
USDA plant hardiness zone: 6
Established: July 6–8, 2007
Front yard exposure: Southwest
Size of front yard: 38 x 40 feet

Design, Materials, and Plants

The design of this regional prototype garden is rational, organized, and rectilinear in deference to the tastes of the owners. The grid also references the nearby grid of Manhattan streets. Surrounding the front yard is a steep slope; it has been planted entirely in strawberries, which will eventually spread to cover it and provide welcoming snacks to neighbors strolling past the house (as well as suspected squirrels and rabbits). Walking up the front steps from the sidewalk you will see that each side of the yard has a different function. On the left is a grid of fifteen raised beds, each 3 x 3 feet, made of recycled black plastic. Between and behind these we have laid down rolls of weed block with black cedar mulch on top. These areas function as low-maintenance paths and, behind, a place for outdoor seating; from this spot the family can enjoy the garden and even eat meals from it.

Each of the fifteen planters contains a different combination of herbs and vegetables, which include:

(1) red lettuces

(2) green lettuces

(3) several varieties of mint

(4) several varieties of basil with cantaloupes, squashes, and zucchinis around the perimeter

(5) eggplants surrounded by a border of alternating varieties of thyme

(6) rhubarb surrounded by leafy greens

(7) climbing cucumbers surrounded by chamomile and catnip

(8) tomatoes surrounded by marjoram and basil

(9) climbing cucumbers surrounded by curry plants and sage

(10) tomatoes with purple basil in the corners and a border of wooly and creeping thyme

(11) an ornamental clipped standard rosemary shrub surrounded by several varieties of mint

(12) lemongrass surrounded by chives and sweet corn

(13) an ornamental clipped standard rosemary shrub surrounded by eggplants and a border of oregano

(14) several varieties of peppers

(15) bok choy with a border of oregano and marjoram

On the right side of the garden as you approach the front door are the fruiting trees and vines. Flanking the sidewalk steps are two dwarf peach trees. You then walk through a series of three arched arbors planted with six varieties of grapes, which will eventually cover them. Aligned with these on the south side are three fruit trees: cherry, apple, and peach. Between each tree is a raspberry bush, which will eventually grow up a six-foot-tall wire tower structure. A circular tiered bed six feet in diameter is densely planted with currants, blackberries, gooseberries, and blueberries. Against the house are grape vines and two potted fig trees, which may be moved inside during especially cold weather.

i come from pennsylvania farm country and my dad's side of the family were all farmers. we had huge vegetable and flower gardens when i was a kid. prior to this house, my husband and i owned an 1850s weekend farmhouse where we grew greens, asparagus, tomatoes, all our herbs, zucchini, rhubarb, carrots, etc., and now that we've moved out of manhattan permanently and found the house we hope to grow old in, i'm thrilled to get my hands in the earth on a daily basis! and can't wait to teach my son the joys of gardening!

i could write forever but i want to get this off asap. please feel free to call me or e-mail for more information or to chat. either way, let me know.
— michelle christman

SOME THOUGHTS A WEEK AFTER PLANTING

Michelle Christman

It's hard to believe that transformation occurred just a week ago. Maybe it's because it seems like a dream; every morning I find myself waking at dawn and looking out my front window to make sure the garden's really there. Or maybe it's because the time I spend each day watering, pulling weeds, pruning, and getting familiar with the plants makes me slow down in a way that nothing else can. Or it could be because we've met more people in the last week than we've met in the past two years because the word is out about our radical project and everyone wants to see it for themselves. Then again, it could be because I've been so busy trying to learn how to become a spokesperson for this type of activism, busy reading up on gardening so I don't let Fritz and the many people who believe in this down by failing to properly tend my garden, busy trying to make a kind of peace with my very unhappy next-door neighbor, and busy speculating about the motive behind the thievery of the Edible Estates sign (my gut tells me it wasn't a random act of vandalism).

I guess it is all of these things combined. But mostly, I think that joy has a way of changing our perception of time. And our garden has already given us more joy than I imagined it could. Sure, we've probably taken on more than we know. But when we watch our son nibble leaf after leaf of cinnamon basil, toss a salad for our parents from just-picked lettuces and herbs that bring back happy childhood memories for my aging father, and brew a pot of fresh mint tea to share with friends who stop by unexpectedly, the work before us doesn't seem so daunting—because the garden will continue to transform us all.

Plants and materials donated by
Gardener's Supply Company

Photography by
Curtis Hamilton for the Canary Project

Thanks to
Volunteer garden workers Isaac Berkowits, Alan Carroll, Kim and Eli Collins, Katherine Coon, Emily Cooper, Joel, Melissa, Elena, and Tallulah De la Fuente, Janet and Julie Gerber, Sara Grady, Curtis Hamilton, Susanna Howe, Svetlana Kitto, Emily Lundberg, Ellie Mueller, Carissa Pelleteri, Fiona Ryan, Ben Salmon, Emily Schroeder, Hugh Snyder, Felix Sockwell, Adam Stolorow, Donna Wingate, and Jason Wood; Andrew Freiband and Sara Grady, for videography; and Dreyer Farms

Maplewood, New Jersey Regional Prototype Garden #3

Edible Estates

a gardenlab project

EDITION FOUR:
LONDON
ENGLAND

LONDON, ENGLAND

The Tate Modern commissioned this garden for Southwark, the neighborhood just to the south of the museum and the river Thames. This area has many council estates (public housing) and happens to be one of the least green parts of the city. After the garden was planted, Edible Estates was included in an exhibition in the Tate Modern's Turbine Hall.

The Edible Estate was established on a highly visible triangular lawn in front of the Brookwood Estate, located a ten-minute walk south of the museum. This rare green space is fenced off and was previously unused. Twenty-four units at Brookwood and another sixteen in Lancaster House (another council estate) all face the triangle. Placing the garden here meant that everyone would be watching: the local gardeners would perform for their neighbors. In the center of the dense city, the production of food would become a public spectacle.

Initially many residents were skeptical about the prospects of such a garden in this location, and they feared it would be vandalized. But there is a school across the street, which ensures a steady flow of children past the garden. It was the children at the council estates who were the most excited about the garden and eager to get their hands in the dirt over the course of the three days of planting.

This garden is intended as a new model for urban agriculture. It is not a true community garden (or "allotment," as the popular practice is referred to in Britain) with separate private plots for each gardener. It is one holistic design that also integrates spaces where people may gather; a pleasure garden made up entirely of edibles. Those who tend it will eat from it.

Estate owners: Tenants of the Brookwood House Council Estate

Location: Southwark, London, England

Commissioned by: Tate Modern

Established: May 25–27, 2007

Size of garden: 31 x 52 1/2 feet

Design, Materials, and Plants

The intricate design for the garden was inspired by the ornate, curvy, raised flower beds that you find in front of Buckingham Palace and Kensington Palace, in Hyde Park, and in most of the Royal Parks in London. The intention was to demonstrate that a place for producing food can also be a beautiful urban amenity. The arabesque shapes allow for easy access to all planting beds and create two oval gathering spaces, one carpeted in turf and the other in gravel; the latter has a ring of tree stumps for seating. The optimal view of the garden is from above; each day the resident gardeners will look down on it from their balconies.

The first planting included a combination of perennial and annual fruits, vegetables, and herbs:

apple trees, to eventually enclose the gravel-paved gathering space

plum trees at the center of our floating "island" garden

various berry bushes, to grow against a brick wall

eggplants

Brussels sprouts

a forest of tomato plants supported by trimmed tree branches

rows of scarlet runner beans, which will eventually cover the small brick structure

peas and sweet peas, which will use small bamboo wigwams for support

lettuce, rocket, chard, and spinach, to cover an entire "wing" of the garden as edible ornamentals

bok choy and fennel, planted in concentric rings around the plum trees

artichokes planted in the center; someday each one could reach over six feet in diameter

onions

an entire bed of parsley and coriander

purple sage

ornamental bay trees trimmed into standards (globes) with corkscrew trunks

an oval of alternating bay and rosemary plants, which will eventually enclose a small lawn for gathering

a row of French thyme surrounding the gravel-paved gathering space

oregano, mint, and basil, to fill out beds along the apple trees and tomato plants

calendula (which produces edible flowers and attracts beneficial insects), arrayed in a row around the oval lawn

marigolds and nasturtiums (these also produce edible flowers) as edging around most of the planting beds

THE MAKING OF A COMMUNAL GARDEN

Carole Wright

"I don't want a garden! I pay my taxes, and I want a car park!" That was the response of one of the residents of Brookwood House, the social housing flats where I—alongside Fritz Haeg and Kathy Noble, assistant curator of *Global Cities*, the exhibition for which the garden was being created—did doorstep consultations for Bankside Open Spaces Trust (BOST), my new employers. Here I was, one week into a new job, with no experience helping to create a garden from scratch—let alone a community garden—working with an artist with a deadline for a museum opening. My three years as a volunteer at BOST had only barely prepared me for the highs and lows of community gardening. How do you prepare someone for working with disenfranchised residents of a block of flats who have a deep mistrust of anyone they see as a figure of authority, have no real sense of community spirit, and haven't had much to do with environmental improvement?

Against that backdrop, and in only one month, we were charged with completing a garden that had the backing of the local authority, Southwark Council, but needed to have the support of the residents. The door-knocking continued for two weeks. We recorded the residents' responses on a questionnaire; over 80 percent were in favor of the garden being created. The one resident who was the most enthusiastic was Denise Withers, who wanted to know if she could come and help right away. She was dying for a chance to get back to working in the community; she'd previously been a youth worker but was unemployed at the time. Even though it was just one resident coming forward, we really needed that type of response because we knew what a slow process it would be to gain the trust and confidence of the other residents. With one person at Brookwood House leading the way, over time we could get others.

Plants were bought from local community gardens, and a poster was displayed inviting people to come and meet Fritz, the curators of *Global Cities*, and me. No one turned up. We kept talking to Denise, she kept talking to other residents, and slowly they started to approach us with their questions. They wanted to know who would look after the garden, and if we would be cutting down the five existing trees. There were so many questions. A date was set to create the garden. It needed to be done in three days. The residents sent their children down to help. Only Denise and one other adult from the neighborhood, Sara Burrows, turned up, along with volunteers from other BOST projects. The housing support officer scoffed that the garden "wouldn't last the weekend," as he handed over a key to a water-supply cupboard. The garden was planted in two days flat with a day to spare.

The challenge was now to keep the residents interested in the garden and help them develop a sense of ownership. It was their garden. I was there, with Denise by my side, every day for the first ten months of the garden's life. The first time there was low-level vandalism by a few children, the parents stepped in and spoke to them. The parents apologized, the children looked shame faced. The garden was already policing itself. Some people let their dogs into the garden, but residents spoke to the dog owners. More questionnaires were issued to ask people how they felt about their new garden and how it could be improved but, more importantly, if they were involved and if not, why. Neighbors who had not spoken to each other for years started having discussions about growing food and gardening in general. They'd talk about okra, yams, plantains, and the merits of growing chard when only one person liked it. They would, and still do, use the garden as a starting point for a wider discussion on their neighborhood and the improvements they want to see. If they can be involved in this, why not in other things?

As for Denise, she is now a seasonal gardener/playworker with BOST. She helps to plan the school's gardening club and works with children from the local primary school in the garden. She visits other neighborhood gardens giving advice on community engagement—and not just related to gardening. It makes me smile when children come up and ask her when the next gardening club event is happening at Brookwood. Denise is aided and abetted by Sara and another local mother, Sharon Reitz. Their love of the garden is evident to all. Their children are growing up with the garden as part of their lives. For them, being part of the garden's life isn't about the awards it's won or its press coverage; it's somewhere they can get some herbs or the odd squash, come to a barbecue, and just sit down to have a good chat.

It still amazes me that this garden, which is on such an exposed site in a very public place, is so loved and respected by the community. Here is this edible oasis in a very urban part of London that has hardly any other green spaces, let alone private gardens. Day in and day out the garden is passed by school children, residents from the neighboring social housing flats, office workers, and many others. They all stop to look at the fruit and vegetables and chat with Denise, Sara, and Sharon, who are the bedrock of the garden. The women are true community gardeners, out there in all weather with their children, answering questions, and harvesting food for their families and passers-by. My

work and life have been enriched by the support of these three. I have learned so much from them, even though my job title is Community Gardener/Educator. Part of my job is to support the garden by arranging volunteer workdays, school gardening clubs, and seasonal events at Brookwood, and they have encouraged neighbors, friends, and family to get involved not only in the garden but other community initiatives as well. Why settle for an environment devoid of green space, living next door to people you don't talk to?

There have been conflicts over where the harvested food goes, how much work people contribute, the occasional visiting dog, or people taking food when they have no connection to the garden. I have a quiet word, and give the involved party information on the next gardening day. It still remains a challenge to keep people interested in the Brookwood garden, and even though, as renters, they are a transitory population, it is vital to involve residents in the neighboring houses. New people come and go, but there is a core of supporters, especially children, who help to maintain it and use it as their hangout.

We'll be celebrating Harvest Festival there soon. Another questionnaire will be done and the answers scanned over to see the direction we should take in the New Year. Recently while Denise and I were talking in the garden, we were approached by one of the residents. He came up to us and said, "I've called my daughter in Ghana, my country, and asked her to send seeds for me to plant in the garden." He is a retired gentleman in his mid-sixties. Two years ago he asked for a car park instead of a community garden. Enough said.

OLYMPIC FARMING 2012

Presented by Fritz Haeg at "Debate London" on June 23, 2007, at the Tate Modern

Every night our London dinner plate becomes the venue for a sort of global Olympic event:

Representing China: Sweet potatoes, traveling 5,000 food miles **From Egypt:** Grapes, at 2,200 miles **Ghana:** Pineapples, 3,100 miles **India:** Bananas, 5,100 miles **Mexico:** Avocados, 5,500 miles **Peru:** Asparagus, 6,300 miles **Saudi Arabia:** Tomatoes, 3,100 miles **South Africa:** Carrots, 6,000 miles **Thailand:** Corn, 5,900 miles **And from the United States:** Apples, 3,700 miles

More than 600,000 Olympic-related guests each day are expected in London for the 2012 summer games. What will they eat? Food that has been grown, sprayed, packaged, and shipped from each of their home countries?

I propose a new extreme summer event: Olympic Farming. Visitors will be served fruits, vegetables, and herbs grown exclusively in the host city. Residents will grow organic food without pesticides or genetic modifications for their guests in every neighborhood across London. Any resident will be able to nominate his or her front garden, or plots of unused public or private land on his or her street, as the site of an official Olympic Farm. Feeding everyone for the Olympic Games will require over 6,000 acres of densely planted gardens. To give you a sense of how much London acreage this is: All Royal Parks total about 4,900 acres; all office space comes to about 4,800 acres; and all common green spaces around flats comprise about 4,200 acres.

Soil on each site will be tested for contaminants, cleaned, and prepared as necessary. This might be a good opportunity to come to terms with our toxic industrial past and the state of the land we live on. A citywide Olympic composting system will be established. Four years' worth of London kitchen scraps will be transformed into the most fertile soil the city has ever seen. An Olympic Farming team will be recruited to represent each neighborhood. Each team will be specially trained to tend one of the thousands of farming venues across the city. They will wear beautiful Olympic Farming uniforms that will be visible from great distances. Everyone will want to be an Olympic Farmer so they can wear the fabulous outfits that are locally customized.

Olympic sponsorship by fast-food chains and soft drink companies will be rejected in favor of this system for a healthy local diet that physically connects visitors to their host. While the Olympics celebrate the gathering of a global community, Olympic Farms will reflect the increasing value of the local. The entire city of London will be radically transformed as empty bits of land, neglected interstitial spaces, rooftops, and even parts of Royal Parks are turned into abundant productive green spaces. All residents of London will watch as agriculture is woven back into the city and public food production becomes a dazzling spectacle.

During the games each Olympic Farm will be open for viewing, tours, and evaluation. Specially designed carts will make visible the movement of the fruits and vegetables the short distance between the host garden and the guest's table. Neighborhood farming teams will be awarded gold, silver, and bronze medals for the quality of their produce and the excellence of their gardens. They will go on to become urban farming superstars, with offers for product endorsements and their faces splashed across the covers of all the tabloids.

After the summer of 2012, London residents will inherit a spectacular network of urban pleasure gardens that will feed them seasonally, instead of empty monumental shells erected for a moment of global vanity. Every evening the children of London (some of whom may not have even known that a tomato comes from a plant) will look at their plates of food that they watched grow down the street and will even know the name of the famous Olympic Farmer who planted it.

Presented at
Tate Modern, June 20–August 27, 2007, as a part of the exhibition *Global Cities*

Partnership and support
Bankside Open Spaces Trust (BOST)

Co-sponsored by
Better Bankside

Land and additional support
Southwark Council

Photography by
Heiko Prigge

Thanks to
Resident volunteer garden workers, including Brooke Blades, Dajana Dokaj, Klaudia Dokaj, Rina Dokaj, Silvia Dokaj, Siobhan Eady, Tiegan Eady, Ben Horrigan, Zoe Horrigan, Fabian McDermott, Denise Withers; community volunteer garden workers, including Jessica Beattie, Joseph Bonner, Sara Burrows, Jill Jerram, Judith Mackinlay, Jeff McMillan, Lily McMillan, Sharon Reitz, Heather Ring, Annina Salo, Reinhard Schleining, Frances Ward, Katie Wright; Michael Osbourne, BOST volunteer; Arthur De Mowbray, for the seating; Mark Barrell, Tenant Liason Officer, Brookwood House Council Estate; Sergio Mutti, Estates Compliance Officer, Brookwood House Council Estate; Carole Wright and Peter Graal, BOST; November Paynter and Kathy Noble, Tate Modern; and Matthew Au, for research and assistance

London, England Regional Prototype Garden #4

Edible Estates

a gardenlab project

EDITION FIVE:
AUSTIN
TEXAS

AUSTIN, TEXAS

One goal of the Edible Estates regional prototype gardens is to demonstrate the possibilities for growing food in front of a variety of housing types. Austin, Texas, is a very progressive city, and in 2008 there were already plenty of examples of front-yard vegetable gardens at single-family homes around town. Apartment buildings surrounded by vacant lawns are a common sight along the periphery of Austin, as they are in cities around the world. Apartment residents may feel they do not have a stake in the open land that is around them; they may even feel unwelcome to initiate gardens on the land just outside their windows.

In response to our announcement searching for an Austin apartment complex to undertake an Edible Estates garden, we heard from the affordable housing providers Foundation Communities. The group's properties primarily serve low-income individuals and families, many of whom were formerly homeless. Foundation Communities also provides children's programs and social services to this population. From its properties, we selected the Sierra Ridge apartment complex as the site for the garden. The 150-unit building was separated from a busy street by a vast open lawn just waiting for something to happen.

Over one weekend in mid-March, around seventy people, both Sierra Ridge residents and local volunteers, descended on the lawn to make a garden. Of the residents who turned out to help plant the garden, most

Estate owners: Sierra Ridge Apartments, Foundation Communities

Location: Austin, Texas

Commissioned by: Arthouse at the Jones Center

USDA plant hardiness zone: 8

Established: March 14–16, 2008

Garden exposure: North

Size of garden: 32 x 50 feet

Design, Materials, and Plants

The garden is an oasis of green space that connects the apartments to the sidewalk. The design of the garden provides places in which to grow food and oval spaces where harvest gatherings and other activities, as well as composting and rainwater catchment, can take place. Each oval is surrounded and framed by a different plant, such as rosemary hedges and fruit trees, to provide a sense of enclosure. The raised beds are made from a combination of locally scavenged rocks and boulders and donated cypress logs. Each space is connected to the next by a narrow path, creating walkways that allow residents to easily tend the crops or simply wander among the plants. It is a social pleasure garden that also happens to produce food for those who tend it.

Central Texas is a very challenging place in which to grow food, especially in the long, hot, dry summer. We planted everything we could find that technically should produce food in this growing zone, with the idea that the residents could see what was possible, what did well, and what they liked to eat, allowing the garden to evolve into a beautiful space they can manage while it also provides sustenance. The residents updated us on what was thriving in the garden in the late summer, eighteen months after the initial planting: rosemary, sage (various varieties), apple, fig, berries (various varieties), persimmon, mandarin, peach, pomegranate, artichoke, tomato, pepper, Indian paintbrush.

STREET

SIDEWALK

UTILITIES

EXISTING PALM

EXISTING LAWN

EXISTING CREPE MYRTLE

EXISTING LAWN

EXISTING CREPE MYRTLE

CEDAR SPLIT LOG RETAINING

FRUIT TREE CIRCLE GATHERING

SPLIT LOG CEDAR RETAIN

EXISTING CREPE MYRTLE

EXISTING SYCAMORE

PARKING

EXISTING SHRUBS

BUILDING

(A) FRUIT TREES · ORCHARD
(B) MOUNDED PLANTINGS OF ANNUAL VEG.
(C) LOW LIGHT ANNUAL GREENS
(D) ANNUAL / PERRENIAL BEDS
(E) PERENNIAL HERB BORDER
(F) COMPOST & RAIN COLLECTION

EDIBLE ESTATE #5: AUSTIN, TX · SCHEMATIC PLAN · 02·19·08
· SIERRA RIDGE ·

0' 3' 7' 15'

were children and teenagers, close to twenty-five of them. Without being asked, they turned out in force to dig holes for trees, shovel dirt, move compost, plant seeds, and rake mulch. This has been true at every Edible Estates garden: the kids are always first on the scene to make the garden, and they are the most optimistic for its future. The land at Sierra Ridge continues today as a communal garden without individual plots, functioning not only as a place in which to gather and produce food but also as an educational space for the children who tend it as it grows with them.

GARDEN REPORT FROM SIERRA RIDGE

Sierra Ridge is an apartment complex in southern Austin owned and run by the Austin-based nonprofit Foundation Communities, which provides long-term, affordable housing solutions. Sierra Ridge has a strong sense of community, and the residents are hard-working, mostly low-income families who take great pride in keeping the buildings and surrounding landscape safe and attractive. Though Austin is home to many community gardens, the expense associated with owning a plot in one is not realistic for most of the Sierra Ridge residents, so they were thrilled when it was selected as the site for Edible Estates Regional Prototype Garden #5. The installation and planting took place over three days with the help of volunteers and residents, many of whom had no previous gardening experience. Some residents initially were uncertain if the garden would survive after the novelty of

its planting had passed. Those doubts have all been erased, and the unique nature of Sierra Ridge has made the garden a giant success. Not every plant from the first season stuck around, but residents have learned which types of produce and herbs can survive the hot Texas summers—such as artichokes, peppers, and rosemary—and which ones will wilt before ripening. Residents truly consider Sierra Ridge home, and because of that, people have planted roots not just in their units but also in the soil on the front lawn. Though most adults at the complex did not take part in the planting, the children of Sierra Ridge turned out enthusiastically to help community volunteers lay the beds and put in the plants. The garden has also caught the eye of more than just those who call Sierra Ridge home. The Travis County Master Gardeners Association has taken an interest in maintaining the garden, and several neighbors in the area have picked out small plots in which to plant their own produce.

Reflecting on the planting, Darrell Gibson, a nineteen-year-old who lives at Sierra Ridge, says, "It was an unforgettable experience. It was fun working on it. . . . I'm glad to have been part of our garden's creation. It's not every day that our community comes together to work on one project as a whole."

Darrell's pride is shared by many of his friends at Sierra Ridge. "I love my garden so much!" shares Lanna Marie Payne, age nine. "We have lots of beautiful plants." Lanna and Darrell both attend Sierra Ridge's after-school learning center and continue to work in and enjoy the garden as part of that program. Their classmate Evelyn Galindo adds, "My experience planting the garden was amazing. We planted mandarins and got dirty; it was fun that I'll never forget. I love working in the garden because you get to be with friends outside, and you get to help the environment."

Sierra Ridge manager Martha Villareal says the garden has helped deepen the sense of community. "Many residents and neighbors told the property managers how wonderful it was to have been selected to plant a community garden on site. The children now know how vegetables actually grow, and they understand that the products they see in the grocery store are there thanks to people who work daily to provide these beautiful vegetables and fruits for their families. We are very fortunate to have the garden, and our residents are very dedicated to maintaining it. Regardless of how hot it gets here, they are in the garden. They love it."

Resident Charles DiTullio, whose apartment looks out directly on the garden, has been involved since day one. After helping with the installation of the garden, he worked with community members and local gardening clubs to bring in new plants and educate his neighbors about gardening, and he even maintains a tool shed outside his apartment to help with the garden's upkeep. "I love the garden," Charles says. "It's such a beautiful view out my window, and I can practically reach out and pull fruit off the trees without leaving my apartment!"

Husband-and-wife team Juan Pescador and Maricela Rodriguez have also taken on the stewardship of the garden. "It's been a great pleasure having the fresh produce from the garden," says Maricela. "I get great joy working in the garden, and my husband also enjoys being involved in tending it. He is a natural gardener; ever since he was a young boy, he has had a green thumb with everything he plants. I assign him the real heavy work, like if a plant needs to have the dirt turned, and he makes sure all the plants are doing well. I find it relaxing to water plants in the evenings, and I like to harvest the vegetables and fruits. When I start supper and I notice I don't have a certain herb, I just look out my kitchen window to see what is out there and then go pick whatever I need," she continues. "I don't have to stop in the middle of fixing supper and go to the grocery store. We've had strawberries, cucumbers, hot peppers, sweet peppers, tomatoes, cilantro, squash, figs, pears, and mandarins. I make soups, salsa, and fresh fruit drinks, all with what the garden has provided."

Presented at
Arthouse, January 26–March 16, 2008, for the exhibition *Fritz Haeg: Attack on the Front Lawn*

Sponsored by
Whole Foods Market

Additional Support
McDugald-Steele, Austin Gardens, Big Red Sun, Jill and Dennis McDaniel, and Melba and Ted Whatley; media sponsorship by *Edible Austin*

Photography by
Sunshine Mathon

Thanks to
Resident and local volunteer garden workers Jon Allison, Ilea Avalos, Mario Badillo, Alpha Balde, Bryan Beltran, Cindy Beltran, Adam Boley, Charles DiTullio, Jennifer Dunnam, Maria Fernandez, Evelyn Galindo, Juliet Gamarci, Claudio Garcia, Jess Garcia, Miguel Garcia, Jeremiah Gardener, Stephen Gardener, Darrell Gibson, Zachary Gibson, Daniella Gomez, Jessica Gomez, Karen Gomez, Maria Elena Gomez, Raymundo Gomez, Ruben Gomez, Rudy Gorostieta, Travis Greig, John Hallock, Barbara Hampson, Brent Hasty, Suzanne Hurley, Julie Killingsworth, Brett Koenig, Elizabeth Lee, Melanie Letot, Karen Lyons, Alexis Martinez, Jess Martinez, Maria Martinez, James Matchett, Tala Matchett, Dan Murphy, Lanna Payne, Wendy Redding, Flo Rice, George Rojano, Dylan Rojas, Zachary Rojas, Oscar Sanchez, Lilia Sanpedro, Travis Seay, Elaine Shen, Ben Slade, Meghan Smith, Sandi Smith, Katie Sternberg, Rachel Tepper, Melissa Torrente, Brian Torrez, Cheyenne Weaver, Ann Williams, Alicia Wong, and Margaret Wong; Melba and Ted Whatley, for their gracious hospitality; Melanie Curiel and Martha Villareal, Sierra Ridge; Christopher Alberts, Sunshine Mathon, and Vicki McDonald, Foundation Communities; Melissa Berry, Elizabeth Dunbar, Jenn Gardner, Sue Graze, Nathan Green, Virginia Jones, Catherine O'Neill, and Caitlin Sweeney, Arthouse at the Jones Center

Austin, Texas Regional Prototype Garden #5

Edible Estates

a gardenlab project

EDITION SIX:
BALTIMORE
MARYLAND

BALTIMORE, MARYLAND

In February 2008 Clarence Ridgley was already starting to think about spring plantings. While searching online for information about berry bushes to plant around the front of his house, he discovered the Edible Estates website on what happened to be the same day we announced a search for a Baltimore family interested in creating the next front-yard prototype garden. At the time, Clarence was tending a few small, raised beds of vegetables in his backyard, and he was starting to think about sneaking some edible plantings in the front, too.

All of the yards on the Ridgleys' street are well tended, and for years Clarence has enjoyed a healthy rivalry with a few of his neighbors, competing for the most luxurious and best-kept front lawn. Announcing his participation in the next Edible Estates regional prototype garden, he informed his local rivals that this year he planned to "blow them all out of the water." After the garden had been established for a few months, it did make quite an impression on the neighbors. Clarence developed new friendships with local residents, sharing some of his produce with them and even allowing a few neighbors to plant their own crops in the space, creating a casual community garden where the Ridgleys' prized front lawn used to be.

Estate owners: Clarence and Rudine Ridgley
Location: Baltimore, Maryland
Commissioned by: Contemporary Museum, Baltimore
USDA plant hardiness zone: 7
Established: April 11–13, 2008
Front yard exposure: East
Size of front yard: 33 x 51 feet

Design, Materials, and Plants

Viewed from the street, the garden has mounded plantings of herbs, vegetables, and fruits on the right. On the left is a circular area for seating, which is surrounded by strawberries and tomatoes, and along the street is a mini-orchard of various fruit trees and a bed of edible flowers. Paths were created with a thick layer of coarse wood chips and bark. The lawn was not removed but instead covered with a thick layer of newspapers—an old gardening trick—upon which the large mounds of rich soil and compost were placed. The newspaper will keep the grass and weeds from sprouting through into the planting areas and will decompose over time. The circular mounded plantings are a simpler, lower-budget, and faster alternative to raised beds and were historically very common among Native American peoples.

The only materials used in the making of this garden were dirt, compost, plants, and mulch. When the garden filled in after a few months, the mounds of dirt and mulch that originally seemed rough or informal were covered by a wide variety of plants. The perennial herbs, berry bushes, fruit trees, and vines became the structure of the garden, as opposed to hardscaping materials, raised beds, or planting structures (apart from one simple bamboo wigwam for the pole beans). The garden is ultimately about the plants, which is all that one could see by the end of the first season.

Plant list:

apples, green beans, beets, blueberries, red cabbage, marigolds, cherries, broccoli, fennel, arugula, grapes, mustard greens, mint, red lettuce, nasturtiums, onions, parsley, pears, green peppers, plums, rosemary, thyme, tomatoes, raspberries, peppermint, spinach, figs, squash, strawberries, oregano

CLARENCE RIDGLEY'S GARDEN JOURNAL

May 16, 2008

I know what the people who pass by our home are thinking: some things are better left unseen. Those tomatoes and cucumbers should be in the backyard, not my front yard. But what's wrong with being different from your neighbors who have a nicely manicured green lawn out front? I have herbs, fruit trees, blueberries, strawberries, tomatoes, grapes, beets, onions, lettuce, arugula, and beans there instead, and in addition to the fruits they are producing, there have been some other unexpected benefits.

I have noticed that traffic slows down in front of my house, like I have my own personal speed bump. Neighbors I had only waved to from a distance as they passed by in their cars now stop or approach me on the street to talk. I often have to put down my garden tools to interact with them. I'm looking forward to a harvest of vegetables, fruits, and new neighborhood friends!

January 4, 2009

Yes, we're doing fine! It is the middle of the winter, and I am beginning to think about the garden this season. I have a head start this year since I have a lot of plants already established. The fruit trees, blueberry bushes, strawberries, grape vines (they grew over forty feet), and herb garden (I'm still using it now in the middle of January) are all doing great, except for one apple tree, which has what looks like a fungus and holes in the buds. I'd like to help it since it's the Golden Delicious, my favorite

apple. Other than that, the fruit trees look like they are all going to produce this year, and I'll actually have to limit the spread of the strawberries. The blueberries have color and look very healthy.

There will be some changes this year. The beets did great last year, and I still have a few jars left. However, I'm the only one in the house who likes them, so I am planning to plant more sweet potatoes instead, though I'm still researching the variety. My family, friends, and neighbors all like the salad mix in the garden, which includes several varieties of lettuce along with onions, peppers, broccoli, tomatoes, and cucumbers. I think I'll move the zucchini and squash to the backyard since they started taking up so much space. I'm also thinking about moving the tomatoes and looking at some varieties not normally seen at places like Home Depot. I plan to replant the edible flower mix to attract back all of the bees that came last year. I've also started a compost bin in the backyard to improve the soil.

March 18, 2009

I started watermelon from seed this year, along with three varieties of tomato: Better Boy, Brandywine, and Early Girl. The salad mix will have various leaf lettuces, such as Romaine and Limestone, along with a wide variety of vegetables, including broccoli, cucumbers, mixed bell and hot peppers, spinach, cauliflower, and red and yellow onions. There will also be eggplants, cabbage, Swiss chard, collards, and squash. I have already planted potatoes, and my wife, Rudine, and I are trying to decide where we should place everything else. I'm not sure if I will plant the watermelon in the front yard, though, because of our two-legged vermin! I remember when I was a kid the fruit was hard to resist, too.

April 19, 2009

The garden did really well over the winter. All of my first-year fruit

Baltimore, Maryland Regional Prototype Garden #6

trees survived. Most of my herbs made it, and my strawberry and blueberry bushes look like they will produce bumper crops this year. There was one challenge of note: Since my garden is in the front yard, it was important to remove plants as they died and maintain as neat an appearance as possible. I also made a record of what grew well and what did not (my collards got a fungus soon after the planting and my cucumbers did not produce very well), and what, as a family, we did not eat (turnips, for instance). I'm making changes this year to correct all of that.

August 31, 2009

This is my second year gardening in the front yard, which I have discovered requires more consideration than the typical backyard plot. Of course, we want to have plants like tomatoes, cucumbers, lettuce, yellow squash, zucchini, and peppers, but after making that decision, the "fun" begins. How can we make our yard colorful and pleasing to the eye so the neighbors aren't stressed about the garden that has replaced the manicured lawn? You should answer such questions before you make the transition to growing food in your front yard. What will your garden look like? How much time are you willing to spend in it? How do you feel about sharing your produce with the neighborhood residents of both the four- and two-legged varieties?

Here is how I approached some of these questions in my own yard: I wanted my garden to have as much variety and to be as colorful as possible in the space I had to work with, so I alternated different-colored plants throughout. I put cauliflower between curved rows of cabbage and placed patches of broccoli and different colors of Swiss chard together around the yard. I made sure to choose varieties of peppers that ripen in different colors. I included both green and red cabbage and planted sweet potatoes around the tomatoes and eggplants.

I did have to spend a lot more time in the garden than I did when it was hidden in back, but if you're a real gardener, you'll know it wasn't work but a labor of love. It paid off. Everything blossomed on schedule, and all I had to do was pull the occasional weed for a few weeks. But then my neighbors took notice. I had a morning routine: I started my day off touring the garden with my cup of coffee. I noticed that a couple of my tomatoes had started to ripen, so I looked for them each morning. One day I decided they would be just right the next morning. That morning I went out with my coffee and saltshaker (no comments about the salt, please). I checked the plant, and the tomatoes had disappeared. As I stood there, my next-door neighbor called to me from her yard and said that she had found two ripe tomatoes, and she hoped I didn't mind that she took them. I had told her that she was welcome to some of my vegetables, I just didn't think she would take my "first born." I found out later that she was inspecting my garden each morning earlier than I was! Excellent crops of cherries and plums also started disappearing.

The good news is that my children's most requested snacks are from the garden. They love the blueberries, strawberries, and grapes. It's fun to watch people pass by the fence and grab a bunch of grapes to eat while walking down the sidewalk. My neighbors stop by frequently for conversation and bags of vegetables. I'm not sure they are all from my neighborhood, but that's okay as long as the conversation and occasional recipe are good.

Here is a list of what you'll find in my front yard right now: Swiss chard, blueberries, strawberries, grapes, bell and hot peppers, eggplant, broccoli, cabbage, cauliflower, sweet potatoes, white potatoes, beets, Brussels sprouts, yellow squash, zucchini, cucumber, tomatoes, figs, borage, and, of course, my herb garden.

What's the best thing about my garden? All of the friends I've made and the plans I have for next year.

Baltimore, Maryland   Regional Prototype Garden #6

Presented at

Contemporary Museum, Baltimore, May 31–August 24, 2008, as part of the exhibition *Cottage Industry*

Sponsored by

M&T Bank; plants sponsored by Green Fields Nursery & Landscaping Company

Photography by

Leslie Furlong

Thanks to

Volunteer garden workers Pam Berman, Jen Brown, Mim Caris, Julie Diewald, Dan Edlavitch, Kenneth Edwards, Mike Fila, Leslie Furlong, Sarah Greenbaum, Karen Hager, Leslie Hatfield, Irene Hofmann, Brennen Jenson, Rebecca Lemos, Paul Maier, Jaimes Mayhew, Nara Park, Ryan Patterson, Kendal Ricks, Chips Shutt, Michelle Simpson, Cynthia Smith, Stuart Smith, Charlotte Walters, Errol Webber, and Shannon Young; Peter Bieneman, Green Fields Nursery & Landscaping Company; Barry Lubinski and the Baltimore City Department of Recreation and Parks, Horticulture Division; Parks and People; High Grounds Coffee; Robert Haywood; Johaniris Rivera Rodriguez; Irene Hofmann, Contemporary Museum, Baltimore

Edible Estates

a gardenlab project

EDITION SEVEN:
DESCANSO
DEMONSTRATION GARDEN
CALIFORNIA

Regional Prototype Garden #7

DESCANSO DEMONSTRATION GARDEN

Descanso Gardens, a 160-acre public garden located at the base of the San Gabriel Mountains, north of Los Angeles, invited Edible Estates to create a public demonstration garden in its featured center-circle planting area for the 2008 calendar year. Unlike the other Edible Estates gardens, this one was tended by a staff of professionals at Descanso, and the food produced was donated to a local food bank. This garden was designed primarily to educate and inspire the thousands of annual visitors, who include local residents, tourists, and gardening enthusiasts.

Adjacent to Pasadena, California, La Cañada Flintridge has a great climate for growing a wide range of plants year round and is home to a very sophisticated and enthusiastic gardening public. The rotating seasonal displays of spectacular ornamental and flowering plants are a highly anticipated feature on the garden's grounds and are especially prominent in the center circle. Since edibles had never before been featured in this space, it was an experiment for Descanso to see if its savvy visitors were ready to welcome a productive landscape into the heart of this typically ornamental area.

A miniature home, consisting of a redwood platform and trellis, was constructed and placed at the center of the garden display. The front

Location: La Cañada Flintridge, California
Commissioned by: Descanso Gardens
USDA plant hardiness zone: 10
Established: January 12, 2008
Size of garden: 35 x 70 feet (oval)

Design, Materials, and Plants

The design and structure of the garden employed a variety of strategies for small-scale domestic food production. Ten-inch-high redwood raised beds, each 4 x 4 feet, lined the front walk and were regularly switched out with annual vegetables and herbs; a domed structure of rebar and tree branches, which people could pass through, was covered with climbing beans, cucumbers, and squash; small paths were created to lead to oval spaces, which were each lined with a different hedgelike perennial herb, including rosemary, thyme, and lavender; a series of five-foot-tall willow branch wigwams was used to create a vertical structure for pole beans to climb; the perimeter of the oval-shaped garden was planted with edible flowers and herbs, such as nasturtiums and creeping rosemary, that would grow to cascade over the retaining wall. The goal was to create a beautiful, food-producing garden that offered many possibilities and ideas for visitors to take home.

Plant list:

Berries: southern highbush blueberries, strawberries (Fragoo white, Fresca, Quinault, Sequoia)

Edible flowers: nasturtiums (Alaska, tall single-bed), marigolds

Fruiting trees and vines: grapes (Black Monukka, Merlot, Ruby seedless), apples (Anna, Fuji, Granny Smith), grapefruits, olives, kumquats, pomegranates, Eureka lemons, Washington navel oranges

Herbs: cilantro, rue, dill, African blue basil, German chamomile, lemon balm, Osaka purple mustard, French sorrel, parsley (curly, flat), tarragon, rosemary, sage, thyme (creeping, Elfin, Pink Chintz, silver, wooly)

Leafy greens: bok choy, mustard greens, lettuce (red rib Italian, Black-Seeded Simpson, green oakleaf, H. Rouge d'Hiver, Outrageous, Red Deer Tongue, red Romaine, Red Sails, Romaine, Ruby), vitamin greens, mache, dandelions, mizuna, arugula, Melody spinach, mixed greens, black kale, Swiss chard (Bright Lights, red)

Vegetables: sugar pea pods, rhubarb, Red Mangel beetroot, Red Acre cabbage, fennel, onions (French red, Green Bunching, Red Delicious), Thumbelina carrots, broccoli, Jade Cross Brussells sprouts, peas (Blauschokker, English), sweetpeas (Bijou, Mammoth)

walk to this "house" divided its "front yard" in half; the left side was planted with a conventional grass lawn, the right side with a complex and dense garden of fruits, vegetables, and herbs. The house served as both a viewing platform and an interpretive center, telling the stories of the two landscapes with signage and graphics oriented out of each of the two windows overlooking the garden and the lawn.

Though some visitors might be familiar with the pleasures of beautiful kitchen gardens, they likely would know them to be placed in backyards, where they are not taken as seriously as the manicured landscapes and gardens in front. By simulating a space that would be very familiar to any homeowner, this Edible Estate garden invited all visitors to consider the choice they have between two very different outdoor possibilities: the lawn or the edible landscape.

The initial planting in January included selected perennial herbs, fruit trees, vines and bushes, and late cool-season greens and vegetables. In May and then again in October, we replanted the garden with featured selections of seasonal vegetables. During the course of just one growing season, visitors could observe the lawn side of the display remain exactly the same, while the garden side changed and evolved dramatically. Beans, squash, edible flowers, and lettuces sprouted and took over their allotted spaces in a matter of weeks. Fruit trees blossomed and bore fruit, and, most dramatically, Italian squash planted at the base of the house covered the garden side of the structure with their huge leaves and pendulous four-foot fruits. Chickens were even brought in every Saturday to spend some time wandering the garden, scratching up the dirt, fertilizing, and eating pests.

The horticulture team measured and recorded the inputs (water, fertilizer, time, fuel) and outputs (food, green waste, biodiversity, air and water pollution) of the opposing garden and lawn and recorded them weekly on a chalkboard chart displayed on the viewing platform. Students from the fourth-grade class at nearby La Cañada Elementary School visited weekly through the spring and fall to investigate this data and, specifically, to observe and record the biodiversity within the garden, including which birds and insects were attracted to the plantings. Their observations, such as this journal entry by Sarah Cooper, age ten, on June 10, 2008, were shared with visitors in display boxes throughout the garden: "Today we went to Descanso Gardens. I can confirm that the Edible Estate sustains more life than the grass area. The plant I am studying is the Red Acre cabbage. It does not have any chewed leaves, but I have noticed approximately ten tiny, yellow eggs right next to it."

Descanso Demonstration Garden *Regional Prototype Garden #7*

GARDEN STORY FROM THE 4TH-GRADE TEACHERS

As fourth-grade teachers at La Cañada Elementary School, we knew it would be an amazing experience for the students to be involved in the new Edible Estates garden—and we were right. It provided a hands-on educational opportunity not easily replicable in the classroom. Every month each of three fourth-grade classes visited Descanso Gardens, measured the growth of plants, tested the soil, weeded, and harvested fruits and vegetables. Students recorded their observations in garden journals with notes, sketches, and even haiku poetry, all related in some way to the year's science curriculum.

Within a short time students began encouraging their families to start their own gardens at home. They also became protective of the exhibit and warned other visiting school groups to stay on the walking paths. The final testimony to our experience occurred during the summer of 2009, when a few fourth-grade graduates voluntarily visited the Edible Estates garden to help harvest the summer vegetables, including gorgeous cucumbers and zucchini. Several of them took vegetables home to share with their families, cementing the idea that edible gardens truly make the most of our natural resources.

—Susan Fuelling, Laurie Hopkins, and Dale Freyberger,
La Cañada Elementary School teachers

Presented at

Descanso Gardens, January 12–December 1, 2008

Thanks to

Rachel Buchwalter, David Brown, Garrett Brown, Travis Fernandez, and Brian Sullivan, Descanso Gardens; Susan Fuelling, Dale Freyberger, Laurie Hopkins, and the fourth-grade class at La Cañada Elementary School

Edible Estates

a gardenlab project

EDITION EIGHT:
LENAPE
MANHATTAN

LENAPE EDIBLE ESTATE: MANHATTAN

This garden landscape is located on a rare patch of open, south-facing land in the middle of Manhattan. The triangular piece of land is in front of Hudson Guild, a vital community center that was established in 1895 and currently serves the 2,000 residents of the surrounding New York Public Housing Authority's Robert Fulton Houses and Elliott-Chelsea Houses. The garden includes the native edible plants and mounded plantings of beans, corn, and squash—also known as the "three sisters"—that the Lenape people would have eaten for millennia in that very location. It provides a view back to their lives and how they lived off the land on the island they knew as Mannahatta at the time that the first European, Henry Hudson, visited in 1609. Unlike the other Edible Estates gardens, which are very much about the present, this garden is a meditation on the historical facts of and future possibilities for our occupation of the island.

The Lenape garden is surrounded by detailed signage that tells the story of each plant, the food it produces, how the Lenape used it in their diet, and the natural history of the site. It is not intended to feed the current local residents, but rather to provide visible evidence of both the general fact that our food comes out of the dirt and specific examples of the sources of food for the previous residents of the island. It is a demonstration garden, part experimental laboratory and

Estate owners: Hudson Guild at Elliott-Chelsea Houses

Location: New York, New York

Produced and presented by: New York Restoration Project in partnership with Friends of the High Line

Founding garden sponsor: Gardenburger LLC

USDA plant hardiness zone: 7

Established: June 13, 2009

Garden exposure: South

Size of garden: 55 x 60 feet

Design, Materials, and Plants

The garden is divided into four distinct zones: woodland, flowering meadow, berry patch, and the "three sisters." Within each there is a variety of edibles, both natives of the island and cultivars of the Lenape. There are no footpaths, and the ground is covered entirely with a combination of wood chips and leaf mulch to approximate the decaying plant material that would have been found on the bottom of a Mannahatta forest. At the center of the garden is a gathering circle—an open space with a ring of tree stumps for seating—which is used as a simple outdoor classroom for visiting student groups.

Plant list:

ZONE 1: WOODLAND
W1 – common persimmon
W2 – red cedar
W3 – American hazelnut
W4 – Solomon's Seal

ZONE 2: FLOWERING MEADOW
FM1 – Butterfly milkweed
FM2 – common milkweed
FM3 – Big Bluestem
FM4 – Jerusalem artichoke

ZONE 3: BERRY PATCH
BP1 – common elderberry
BP2 – highbush blueberry
BP3 – lowbush blueberry
BP4 – wild strawberry
BP5 – raspberry

ZONE 4: "THREE SISTERS"
TS1 – corn
TS2 – beans
TS3 – squash

part educational display. Visiting students and those from the nearby children's center use the garden and its central gathering circle for activities and workshops dealing with the history, ecology, food, plants, animals, energy, and other aspects of the immediate natural environment.

The residents of Elliott-Chelsea Houses, members of the Hudson Guild community, visiting students, and the general public become more aware of organic growing cycles as they watch the garden evolve through the seasons and years. They become aware of the natural and cultural history of the island they live on by observing food growing on plants that existed in Manhattan soil before it was the city we know today. This garden landscape may also serve as a model for small-scale urban edible landscapes and as a possible prototype for modest green spaces at similar housing sites across the city.

ZONE 1: WOODLAND

Common persimmon *Diospyros virginiana.* In the fall this tree produces an orange fruit that the Lenape people harvested and stored. Molasses can be made from the fruit's pulp, a tea can be made from its leaves, and the roasted seeds can be used as a substitute for coffee beans. Unripe fruit and the plant's inner bark have been used for various medicinal purposes.
Red cedar *Juniperus virginiana.* The berries of red cedars were eaten and also used in sweat baths, along with sage and mint leaves and goldenrod flowers. Wood from this tree was used to make poles that marked agreed-upon tribal hunting territories.
American hazelnut *Corylus americana.* The half-inch-diameter nuts are enclosed in a hairy husk with ragged edges, and they ripen from green to brown in late summer. These nuts were crushed and used by Native Americans as a base for soup or eaten raw with honey. Tribe members drank a tea made from the inner bark to cure hives and hay fever.
Solomon's Seal *Polygonatum biflorum.* The rhizome, or rootstock, of this plant served many functions. It was eaten as a source of starch (after being cooked overnight in lye water to remove its bitterness), ground into a flour to make bread, steamed and inhaled to treat headaches, burned for fragrance, made into a medicinal tea, and poulticed to treat skin ailments.

ZONE 2: FLOWERING MEADOW

Butterfly milkweed *Asclepias tuberosa.* All of the aboveground portions of the plant were cooked and eaten, and the roots had several medicinal uses. Some Native American legends recount the roots being used as a bodywash to improve lifting and running strength. The bark was also used to make a strong fiber that was then made into twine and cloth.
Common milkweed *Asclepias syriaca.* During the spring some Native American peoples cooked the young shoots, eating them as an asparagus-like food. As a root tea, common milkweed also had medicinal uses for a number of respiratory, digestive, and joint conditions. The high dextrose content of its nectar led to milkweed's use as a sweetener. This plant, especially the root, is considered toxic without sufficient preparation or when consumed in large quantities.
Big Bluestem *Andropogon gerardii.* Bluestem grass was valued for its mold-resistant properties; it was used to line beds and

storage pits dug in the soil. A tea made from the leaves was used as a wash to relieve fevers. Big Bluestem once dominated the tall-grass prairies of North America but was largely replaced by the corn and wheat crops that came with European settlement.

Jerusalem artichoke *Helianthus tuberosus*. This plant produces a beautiful sunflower in late summer and potato-like tubers that can grow to two inches in diameter. The Lenape dug out the tubers, dried them, and pounded them into flour; they also baked whole tubers in underground ovens.

ZONE 3: BERRY PATCH

Common elderberry *Sambucus canadensis*. The blue and purple elderberries are edible and high in vitamin C, though the red berries of other species are toxic. Native Americans made juice and tea for babies from elderberry flowers. The berries and flowers were also used for medicine and dyes, while the stems were used as twirling sticks for starting fires.

Highbush blueberry *Vaccinium corymbosum;* **lowbush blueberry** *Vaccinium angustifolium*. The Lenape used all parts of the plant and were especially fond of eating wild blueberries for sustenance; they dried them for year-round nourishment. They also used the berry for dyes and medicinal purposes. Native American legend tells of a Great Spirit that sent the "star berries"—a reference to the star-shaped structure at the bottom of the blueberry—to relieve famine.

Wild strawberry *Fragaria virginiana*. The wild strawberry was used extensively and considered sacred by many Native Americans. Their style of crushing the fruit and eating it with baked cornmeal bread inspired the colonists' creation of strawberry shortcake. The Mohawk name for strawberry, *noon tak tek hah kwa*, means "growing where the ground is burned," which refers to the appearance of berry patches in meadows that flourished after brush burnings.

Raspberry *Rubus idaeus*. In addition to gathering and eating the berries, the Lenape also made tea from the plant's leaves. The tea has a long medicinal history as an astringent, as well as a treatment for wounds, diarrhea, and colic pain. Red raspberry is a member of the rose family, native to Europe and Asia, though North America is the naturalized habitat of several subspecies.

ZONE 4: "THREE SISTERS"

Corn, beans, squash. The Lenape people practiced multicropping with the traditional "three sisters" garden, growing corn in combination with beans and squash. Beginning in late April, Lenape men cleared a plot of land by felling the large trees and burning the vegetation. The burning fertilizes the soil with ash, which promotes plant growth by changing the soil chemistry from acidic to alkaline and releasing more nutrients. In early May the women created dirt mounds and planted a circle of corn kernels saved from the year before. A few weeks later, they planted beans around the corn stalks and squash around the rest of the mound. Over the course of the summer the tall corn stalks provide a structure for the beans to climb. The beans have nodules on their roots that transform nitrogen from the atmosphere into a natural fertilizer that feeds the corn and squash. Meanwhile the shade of the large green squash leaves keeps the weeds down and holds in soil moisture between rain showers (the Lenape didn't practice irrigation). Crops were harvested from late summer until the first frost, usually in October.

A BRIEF ACCOUNT OF THE FOOD HABITS OF THE LENAPE OF MANNAHATTA

Eric W. Sanderson

Everyone needs to eat. All societies in all places at all times must find ways to provision food; it's as fundamental to economics as it is to ecology. Today New York City is world-renowned for its food, which is collected from all over the world, prepared in myriad manners, and then exchanged for paper and plastic money in famous restaurants and cafés. But what about before there was a city, money, or cafés? What about when the land was green with trees and covered with hills, when sparkling streams wound through wetlands and across fields down to the fertile, productive estuary surrounding the island? What were the food ways of the first New Yorkers?

For nearly a decade my colleagues and I at the Wildlife Conservation Society have been working to rediscover the ecology of New York when Henry Hudson, the first European explorer, arrived in September 1609. The results, presented in the Mannahatta Project, tell, in part, the story of food on the island. On Mannahatta (the original Lenape name for Manhattan, meaning "island of many hills") many different societies found good food to eat—all of it slow and local, collected on the island or in its surrounding waters. One can imagine a society of squirrels finding nuts among the oak and chestnut trees of the Upper East Side, porpoises hunting for bluefish in the harbor just off the shore of Tribeca, and societies of ferns slowly accumulating sunlight in the shade of woodlands in Washington Heights. In all these neighborhoods, energy and materials passed along food webs, originating from the sun, atmosphere, and soil, eventually reaching the physical bodies of living creatures, and then passing through them back to the soil and atmosphere. And what was generally true for populations of squirrels, porpoises, ferns, and many other organisms was also true for Mannahatta's people.

When Henry Hudson arrived in 1609, he found Native Americans of the Lenape culture—the "real people," as they knew themselves. The Lenape extended from southeast New York across most of New Jersey to the Delaware Bay and into eastern Pennsylvania. They were considered by other northeastern peoples of the Contact Era the "Ancient Ones" of Algonquin culture. The Lenape told the story of how the North American continent was formed on the back of a turtle. They built curvilinear, wooden homes from the living materials of the forest. And they ate food that was diverse, nutritious, and surprisingly abundant.

Food on Mannahatta followed the seasons, and the Lenape followed the food. In April and May they moved their camps to the water's edge to take advantage of the fish runs, when millions of shad and other herring, trout, and sturgeon surged up the rivers, seeking their breeding waters upstream. The Lenape caught them with nets and fish traps and spent hours drying the fish over smoky fires on the beaches that lined the west side of the island, from today's Battery to Forty-second Street.

In early summer the Lenape moved inland to places suitable for growing gardens, usually near their wigwams and longhouses, which were beside permanent sources of fresh water. To start a garden they cleared a field by cutting trees and starting fires, then they formed the soil into mounds on which they would plant the three traditional sister crops of Native America: corn, beans, and squash. Our research shows that the beans fed the

corn with nitrogen, the corn provided a scaffold on which the climbing bean plants could grow, and the squash extended its large leaves to shade the soil, limiting the weeds and minimizing evaporation. Along the margins of their plots, the Lenape also grew sunflowers and tobacco and cultivated Jerusalem artichoke and other wild plants.

In the forests around them, they collected herbs, roots, nuts, and berries as these foods came in season. Mannahatta offered blueberries, blackberries, elderberries, nannyberries, gooseberries, straw-berries, and wild grapes. In the fall many of the trees produced abundant nut crops—chestnuts, hickory nuts, beechnuts, and acorns. The Lenape also hunted the many mammals, birds, and reptiles in the forests, including wild turkeys, snapping turtles, deer, and perhaps elk. Black bear was considered a particular favorite, providing not only meat but, more important, grease with which to cook and cover their bodies, and thick, warm fur to use for clothing and blankets during the cold months.

In the winter the Lenape lived off of dried fish, nuts, corn, beans, and squash, often storing the food in small pits they dug in the ground and lined with bluestem grass. They continued to hunt and fish and, when food ran low, to collect the harbor's plentiful oysters, clams, mussels, and even lobster. Analysis of the bones of Mannahatta's inhabitants shows that their diets were slanted toward seafood, and no doubt the year-round abundance of sedentary shellfish offshore provided a reliable food supply.

Fritz Haeg and his partners and volunteers created the Lenape Edible Estate at Twenty-sixth Street and Tenth Avenue, but 400 years ago that block was dominated by American chestnuts, in a rich, moist forest with oaks and tulip trees, which sloped down a hillside toward the nearby Hudson River shore. One could have stood in the block and, listening carefully, heard the lapping waves of the river on the beach halfway between Tenth and Eleventh Avenues. Two streams met in the block, which meant that, in addition to hunting for white-tailed deer, wild turkey, and passenger pigeons, one also might have fished for brook trout and American eel. Gathering Lenape may have found hawthorns, groundnuts, huckleberry, and mayflower fruit, among other plants.

Given the abundance of food in Manhattan's grocery stores and restaurants and the largely invisible ways that food is delivered from all over the world to the city today, it sometimes is hard to believe that once upon a time people grew, collected, and prepared all the food they ate directly on the island where they lived. It is easy to forget that under the asphalt of Tenth Avenue there is soil; and though rain still falls on the city today, it is considered a problem, not a virtue. But if that soil was released from its stony tomb, it could grow food again. And if the rainwater wasn't diverted to storm drains, it could create new streams. That is why I think the work Fritz and his partners have done with the Lenape Edible Estate in Manhattan is important: to remind us of our geographical past and to suggest the promise of our geographical future—in New York City and elsewhere—so once again we will know, as the Lenape did, where our food comes from.

Produced and presented by
New York Restoration Project in partnership with Friends of the High Line

Founding sponsor
Gardenburger LLC

Photography by
Oto Gillen

Signage design by
PS New York

Landscape ecology consultant
Eric W. Sanderson, Wildlife Conservation Society, The Mannahatta Project, themannahattaproject.org

Thanks to
Volunteer garden workers Miriam Bergen, Carly Berwick, Lola Bloom, Claudia deLuna Castro, Chloe Cerwinka, Abigail Cooney, N Dash, Nicole Fitzgerald, David Freudenthal, Sarah Johnson, Renee Kaufman, Bettina Korek, Cathy Lebowitz, Rebecca Lemos, Kristin Mann, Diana Murphy, David Nimowitz, Elizabeth Oh, Veronica Perretti, Stephanie Porto, Mimi Slaughter, Kol Solthon, Allison Walwyn, Corinne Weiner, and Laura Zuspan; special thanks to Kris Slava, Ovation; Bettina Korek and Karen Marta, ForYourArt; Robert Hammond, Peter Mullan, and Danya Sherman, Friends of the High Line; Meghan Barrier, Drew Becher, Christopher Drury, Amy Gavaris, and Simon Skinner, New York Restoration Project

Edible Estates Attack on the Front Lawn 143

We put out a call looking for people across the country who have made their own front-yard Edible Estates, inviting them to submit stories of their experiences and photographs of the results. Here are some of the best examples from a diversity of regions and climates, denoted by the United States Department of Agriculture hardiness zone classification. They are accompanied by planting calendars for each zone.

REPORTS FROM COAST TO COAST

ZONE 10

Location: Los Angeles, California
Yard size: 18 x 20 feet
Established: 2003

Grass is just not our thing. Sod is for sickos. Lawns are for losers. We moved into a bungalow in South Los Angeles in the fall of 2003. The front yard was full of grass, mature jade plants, and fussy flowers. There were two cypress trees joined in an embrace to welcome visitors through our oversized metal gate and into someone else's garden fantasy.

We ripped out the fence. We let the grass die and then killed the roots and every other living thing with a black plastic lawn shroud. This kill-em-all-let-god-sort-em-out attitude worked. We dug out the jade. We sawed the cypress. We cut our hands too many times on the roses before showing them who was boss of the yard. And then we called Francisco over with his crew for some extreme rototilling.

Now our lawn is a vegetable garden. We have vegetables in pots, in barrels, in the ground, and in an L-shaped raised bed. The original idea was to have them all reside in the raised bed, but our greed for tomatoes and Italian beans got the best of us, and the garden started growing anywhere there was some available dirt.

One of the best things about having a garden is the ability to grow vegetables that are otherwise unavailable. Louis's family brought purple pole beans and hot peppers from the Calabrian hills to Canada in the early 1960s. His family has been growing them ever since, and we are ecstatically continuing the tradition on our edible estate. This year the beans tower above heirloom zucchinis (from Susan Lutz's family in Virginia), tomatoes of all varieties, cucumbers, herbs, and, importantly, the Calabrian peppers.

The garden is always changing. Last year we grew sunflowers, including the sixteen-foot Sunzilla. The year before we gave over half the lawn to a corn crop, which soared from the earth and thrilled everyone who walked by. During other times of the year we have peas and kale and Swiss chard and lettuce.

Our backyard is mostly concrete. This year Francisco returned with a jackhammer to reveal a strip of rich dirt, which became the home to three citrus trees, some basil, and a few pepper plants. We have tomatoes growing back there, too, next to the compost piles.

– Lisa Anne Auerbach and Louis Marchesano

ZONE 10

Location: Pasadena, California
Yard size: 2 beds, 4 x 5 feet each
Established: 2006

I decided to plant in my front yard because I didn't want to take up any more of our backyard space and our front yard got great sun. However, my family discovered that we didn't even know the best reason, which was that our garden has become a focal point of community for our neighborhood.

People are always stopping by. We put the garden in only five months after moving into our neighborhood. We had been on the margins of several relationships, when suddenly people began coming by constantly to talk about the garden. I am now out front often, bumping into people, especially kids, who particularly love it. It is hard to convey the degree to which our garden has become a fixture of our neighborhood and our conversations.

Whether it's the fifty-something woman walking by who is moved to tell me her memories of her mother's garden in Austria and later waters my garden while I'm gone, or the struggling actor two doors down who just thinks the whole thing is "cool" and now wants to grow a giant pumpkin, or the kids that started picking strawberries and have begun asking for cucumbers and beans, my garden has grown into something on our block more valuable than vegetables.

We grow a little bit of everything. I seek to find the most flavorful, beautiful varieties of any vegetable, and it thrills me to look at my garden filled with gray shallots, black tomatoes, pink garlic, yellow cucumbers, purple artichokes, striped beans, and lavender eggplants.

Our life is richer for a vegetable garden, especially one in the front yard!

– Christopher Brandow

ZONE 09

Location: Sacramento, California
Yard size: 28 x 40 feet
Established: 2008

It all started by feeling dissatisfied with our front yard and mourning the time we spent laboring over the lawn. Our family thought about the wasted water, the lawnmower emissions, and the valuable space. In 2007 the Sacramento city codes were changed to allow for front-yard vegetable gardening; and so in December 2008, inspired by the first edition of *Edible Estates*, we took action. I reasoned that our region's rainy season was a good time to dig out the grass because the ground was so soft—and I was too impatient to wait for better weather—but it meant that I was out in the rain making a muddy mess. It was ugly in the early stages, which involved moving dirt and creating mounds to define the garden areas. I apologized to neighbors and pacified them with promises of shares of the summer harvest.

The garden generated much interest among friends and members of our community, and at first I was a little nervous and self-conscious. People remained skeptical until early summer, when the plants started to fill in and the garden really began to take shape. On many occasions we abandoned our shovels to talk with passersby, answering questions like: "What are you doing?" "What happened to the lawn?" and "Can I do this at my house?" Some people warned me that a front yard garden would be "a liability," which to this day I don't fully understand, and others said I was setting myself up for too much work. Cars drove by, and I could see frowns and confused glances from the drivers. But as the plants grew and blossomed, so did my confidence, and soon people began offering encouragement and suggestions. Now people often yell from their car windows, "I love your yard!" or they stop long enough for me to pass them a handful of produce.

We have two rules for our garden: we only grow edibles or plants that attract pollinators, and we maintain the space organically. We grow herbs, tomatoes, onions, summer and winter squash, corn, lettuce, and potatoes. There is something in every corner every season. Not only do we grow enough produce to nourish our own family, but we also have plenty to share with friends and neighbors. It is remarkable that cultivating vegetables is also cultivating a sense of community.

— Beth Olagues

Location: Austin, Texas
Yard size: 20 x 12 feet
Established: 2007

I'd like to tell you that my decision to go edible came after some kind of revelational experience, but it was actually more of a gradual realization that most people living in and around urban areas were not making very good use of the land surrounding their homes. And it wasn't any one particular reason that convinced me to landscape my yard with edibles. In fact, any of the tens of reasons I could name is highly compelling. To me, landscaping with edible (or at least consumable) plants seemed like the only sensible thing *to do* with the little patch of earth surrounding my humble abode.

When my wife and I started looking for our first house in Austin, Texas, one of the features at the top of my list was "big yard with plenty of open space." Sure, that's what a lot of young couples with children (and/or dogs) probably say they want, but I wasn't thinking about canines or kids—for me it was garden or bust. It was my plan to try something that some people call "edible landscaping."

Well, how is that any different than just planting a patch of veggies in the corner of the backyard, you might be asking? Edible landscaping is a form of urban agriculture, but it is different in that it consistently places as much or more emphasis on aesthetic considerations as it does on consumable yields. My edible landscapes usually consist of a variety of fruits, vegetables, and herbs combined with colorful annual flowers.

Even though my Edible Estate started off as a personal project, I have helped dozens of people in my community to start transforming their yards into edible oases—and it's been one delicious experience after another!

— **Justin Bursch**

Location: East 29th Street (unofficial) coop, Austin, Texas
Yard size: 25 x 20 feet and 6 x 10 feet
Established: 2007

Our front yard is now a jungle. Vines are creeping in the front door. We've come a long way in just eight growing months from literally lifeless to fantastically fertile grounds. We dug our front lawn up for our winter garden last year. The soil was barren, rock-hard, dry, and dusty. About 450 square feet were pick-axed, tilled, de-rocked, and weeded, with a little manure added, then planted, all in a week's time. The heat of Texas's August gave us all sunburned necks and blistered fingers. We read and talked to pros about organic methods, companion planting, crop rotation, etc. We integrated aesthetically pleasing as well as functionally efficient design.

Since planting our front yard, we have made friends with all of our neighbors. Bradley, a middle-aged artist, dumps his coffee grinds and kitchen scraps in our compost, borrows fresh parsley from our herb border, and in return gives us fresh-made chutney. Chris, another neighbor, helped us dig. So when wild tomato plants show up, we give him some for his backyard, along with summer squash seeds my grandmother dried herself. Carrie right next door donated a dying pallet of chives that is now fireworking from the earth and whose cuttings go straight into savory soups and sautéed kale dishes we make for dinner. People walking by say, "I LOVE your garden." The toddlers at the daycare center across the street always ask, "What are you doing?" and "Why you doin' that?" and we say, "Gardening...so we can EAT!"

We planted our smaller bed in the "three sisters" tradition. Our compost heap is going wild with potatoes, pumpkin, and tomato. We eat the Chinese kale flowers right off the plant and chew spearmint leaves for a cool refreshing burst. Nothing is more satisfying than sitting outside at dusk, smelling the greenness you have cultivated, watching fireflies light up like they do in forests, contemplating your full belly thanks to all the edible wonders that water, sun, moon, and soil have brought right into your front yard.

– J Muzacz

Location: Narbeth, Pennsylvania

Yard size: L-shaped bed, each arm 4 x 15 feet, and side bed, 50 sq. feet

Established: 2006

My husband and I are living in the middle of a small suburban town in Pennsylvania, within sight of the post office. We are only renting, but our landlords let us rip up the grass and put in an organic front-yard vegetable garden. We tilled in compost and composted sheep manure from a friend's farm. We planted flowers and strawberries near the sidewalk, and a large assortment of heirloom vegetables closer to the house. We had three kinds of tomatoes, bell peppers, two types of hot peppers, bush beans, lettuce, carrots, baby watermelon, amaranths, herbs, cucumbers, nasturtiums, and marigolds. We were concerned that the neighbors would be bothered by the slightly less manicured appearance, but almost every person who walks by stops to chat when we are outside working. One elderly man worked for Heinz for his entire career and loves to talk about tomatoes. Another woman broke her back years ago and can no longer garden except in containers, and she often comes by to check on our progress. We did not have time to can last year, so when the Brandywines came in faster than we could eat them, the neighbors got to taste the fresh-from-the-vine tomatoes. When people saw us putting in peas, carrots, and lettuce a few weeks ago, they all stopped to find out what we were planting this year. We did not intend for this project to build community, but people love edibles!

Last year, our landlords, who live in the building, too, had corn along the sidewalk on one side of the house and their own backyard garden. We have already torn up more of the yard this year for more beds, which are a combination of flowers, herbs, and about a dozen more varieties of vegetables. We will also be putting in several kinds of berry bushes, and possibly grapes. I would encourage anyone who can landscape with edibles to try this. I actually think being in the front yard helped our garden's health—we walked by it all the time and noticed when any plants were struggling (which wasn't often, due to companion planting and excellent soil). This was actually our first garden, and we had tremendous success and learned many lessons that we will put to good use this year.

— **Leah Swann**

Location: Richmond, Virginia
Yard size: 28 x 20 feet
Established: 2007

February 2007. The piece of paper in front of me looked something like this:

Pros: Two flat 14 x 20 foot plots of land; south-facing; full sun all day; I'll see the garden every day as I walk out my front door.

Cons: Everyone else will see the garden every day as they walk past my front door.

It wasn't so much a "con" as an uncertainty. An edible front yard would be good stewardship of the little piece of land that I have. Could the "con" of high visibility actually be a "pro"? I swallowed my doubt.

March arrived. I borrowed my neighbor's tiller, turned my yard into a plot of dirt, and panicked momentarily as I passed the "point of no return." I laid out a walking path, cultivated beds, put in herb borders, and planted seeds.

At the very least, the resulting garden is a talking point. It piques curiosity. I've met more folks in the neighborhood in the last four months than I have in five years. Some ask questions. "What's that plant?" "Are squash and zucchini hard to grow?" Most offer words of encouragement. "I love walking by every day and seeing the progress." "I really believe in what you're doing." "Looks fantastic—keep up the good work!"

In truth, I'm an amateur. Last year was my first attempt at growing vegetables. It started as a pastime, a fun novelty: vegetables to which I could lay claim from my own ground. In a short time, it has raised my awareness of the origins of what I eat, made me more intentional about choosing food. More than that, though, I feel intimately connected with the earth. Watching a seed emerge from its burial to grow into a plant larger than my arms' reach—and being an active participant in this natural cycle—has evolved into a tangible expression of faith in the natural order of things. That it produces the same fruitful results over and over again, year after year, is nothing short of miraculous. That I can share this with others in my own front yard is the icing on the cake.

– Chris Edwards

ZONE 06

Location: Needham, Massachusetts
Yard size: 20 x 20 feet
Established: 1968

Over thirty-five years ago, my husband decided that vegetables were prettier than grass, and you didn't have to mow them! We moved here and he thought the property was very beautiful when we came to look at it. The house takes up a small part of the property, and the front, both sides, and back were augmented by what we called "the back forty." I suppose he thought grass stopped growing at a certain point, having lived in cities all his life, from Budapest to New York.

At about that time, a neighbor loaned me his copy of Ruth Stout's *How to Have a Green Thumb Without an Aching Back: For the Aging, the Busy and the Indolent*. We hired a boy to dig a garden for us, not in the front lawn, but on the side. He thought that 10 x 20 feet was about right. After tomatoes and beans went in, there was still lots of grass to be mowed. Ruth Stout's method was to cover everything with hay. In her book she wrote about a woman who read her book and went out to a meadow, put the potatoes on the grass, and covered them with hay. I had some potatoes in my cellar refrigerator that

had sprouted, so I did the same thing. Right next to the dug bed, I marked off another 10 x 20 feet, so my garden looked 20 x 20. Not having hay, but having lots of grass, I covered the potatoes with dried grass and kept adding more as they grew. The potatoes were great. BUT the most important thing that happened was that after digging up the potatoes, I had a 20 x 20 foot patch for next year's garden. The following year I used potatoes that I deliberately bought for sprouting and doubled the garden again. The only thing was to watch out for potato plants, so I planted things that grew up each year in last year's potato patch.

TIP FOR TODAY: Use potatoes to dig your garden for you. You might want to buy seed potatoes, since I don't think they sprayed store-bought potatoes in 1968!! Yup, that's when I started MY EDIBLE ESTATE!

— **Dorothy Stark**

ZONE 05

Location: Chicago, Illinois
Yard size: 25 x 35 feet
Established: 1995

After living in cramped city apartments, I moved with my husband and two children into our first home: an 1893 farmhouse on the north side of Chicago. Once I got my hands in the dirt there was no turning back. It didn't matter that the house needed painting, the roof needed fixing, or the gang kids on our street corner needed reprimanding; my energy was focused on the wildly overgrown front lawn. My goal was to replace the browning, brittle grass and sadly drooping bushes with an exuberant, eye-catching, densely textured vegetable garden that had visual interest through the seasons, making this precious land as productive and efficient as possible.

I observed the sun exposure, studied the space, drew diagrams, and developed a design featuring a maze created by paths and beds that leads to the center of the garden. I used scavenged bricks to build the raised beds, cobblestones for the maze's paths, and cedar for the trellis, which supports the tomatoes, hardy kiwi, and grape vines and maximizes the use of the space. I continue to build up the soil with kitchen scraps, grounds from coffeehouses, and compost from manure from city horse stables.

What was once a wasted plot of barren soil is now abundant with vines of black raspberries, blueberries, grapes, hardy kiwis, loganberries, and currants. Vegetables include kale, peppers, beans, lettuce, arugula, Jerusalem artichokes, and tomatoes. Basil, sage, savory, chives, lavender, tarragon, parsley, rosemary, oregano, and lemongrass represent the herbs. Not only has my garden been a great source of nourishment for my mind and body, but it also has been a draw for insects, birds, and neighbors! People passing by seem to notice how the garden changes through the seasons. Our urban vegetable garden has become a neighborhood destination.

I cannot imagine a life where I am not able to sink my hands in the dirt and witness the drama of the annual cycle of a seed turning into a plant, which grows a vegetable, which creates more seeds. The garden grounds me, and as an artist and a cook, it connects these two aspects of myself. Sometimes tending it feels like the most important thing that I do. Oh, and did I mention that I also have a backyard?

– Barbara Cooper

Location: Montpelier, Vermont
Garden size: 2 beds, 3 x 70 feet each
Established: 2009

No front lawn in all of Vermont is more visible or more prized than that of the State House in Montpelier. Long known for its colorful flower displays and used by local residents as a site for playing Frisbee, running with dogs, and watching fireworks on the Fourth of July, the lawn became host to a new attraction on May 14, 2009, when it was planted with a vegetable garden, the first such garden on any state capitol lawn in the nation.

The Vermont State House Food Garden is the handiwork of the APPLE Corps (Association for the Planting of edible Public Landscapes for Everyone), a small citizens' group that formed in the cold snowy days of January 2009. While adding to the beauty and symmetry of the formal lawn, the garden was intended to inspire and educate Vermonters to grow more of their own food both at home and in other spaces, including community, corporate, county, state, and federal lawns. It was also intended to feed people. By midsummer of its first season, the garden had yielded more than 200 pounds of lettuce, Swiss chard, collards, kale, peas, cabbage, and beets, all of which went to a local food pantry and soup kitchen.

While the APPLE Corps launched the garden plan with a band of just seven volunteers, the effort quickly gained the wholehearted support of the state government, local businesses, and schools. As the project got under way, community merchants donated garden tools and equipment; seed companies and local farms donated seeds and seedlings; and a class from Montpelier High School nurtured 150 lettuce starts. Vermont legislators and representatives from the Vermont Agency of Agriculture attended the dedication ceremony, and many took the opportunity to plant some of the first seeds.

At approximately 420 square feet, the State House Food Garden is small in size, but since it stretches for 140 feet on the front lawn, it is a prominent space that has been seen and admired by tourists, legislators, and other visitors. The APPLE Corps hopes that the garden will inspire Vermonters and other Americans to dig up their own front yards to plant vegetable gardens and fruit trees. It's the ultimate vision for a twenty-first-century victory garden!

– Glenn Scherer and the APPLE Corps

Regional Planting Calendars

USDA PLANT HARDINESS ZONE MAP OF THE U.S. MAINLAND

ZONE	Average Annual Minimum Temperature Range per Hardiness Zone and Some Edibles That Will Grow	Hardneck Garlic	Black Currants	Horseradish	Dandelions	New Zealand Spinach	Reliance Peaches	Bee Balm	Chamomile	Florence Fennel	Jerusalem Artichokes	Lemon Balm (Melissa)	Eastern Prickly Pears	Garden Sage	Flowering Quince	Nashi (Asian) Pears	Anise Hyssop	Sea Kale	Loganberries	Wreath Nasturtium	Chinese Pistachio	Loquats	Rosemary	Passion Fruit	Pomegranates	Kumquats	Siamese Ginger	Aloe Vera	Avocados	Blood Oranges	Cherimoyas	Star Fruit	Dragon Fruit	Tamarillos	Tomatillos
10	30 to 40 F				•								•	•					•		•	•	•	•	•	•	•	•	•	•	•	•	•	•	•
09	20 to 30 F		•	•										•					•		•	•	•	•	•							•			
08	10 to 20 F	•	•	•	•	•	•	•	•	•	•	•	•	•	•	•	•	•	•	•	•	•	•		•										
07	0 to 10 F	•	•	•	•	•	•	•	•	•	•	•	•	•	•	•	•	•	•	•	•		•		•										
06	-10 to 0 F	•	•	•	•	•	•	•	•	•	•	•	•	•	•	•	•	•	•	•	•														
05	-20 to -10 F	•	•	•	•	•	•	•	•	•	•	•	•	•					•																
04	-30 to -20 F	•	•	•	•	•	•	•	•	•	•	•	•	•	•																				
03	-40 to -30 F	•	•	•	•																														

ZONE 10

REGIONAL PLANTING CALENDAR
Victorville, California; Naples, Florida; Coral Gables, Florida; Miami, Florida

Plant seeds in:	Winter Zucchini (†)	Watermelons (†)	Turnips (†)	Tomatoes (†)*	Swiss Chard (†)	Sunflowers (†)	Sweet Potatoes (†)	Strawberry (+)	Squash, Winter (†)	Squash, Summer (†)	Spinach (+)	Rutabagas (†)	Roquette (+)	Radishes (+)	Pumpkins (†)	Potatoes (†)	Peppers (†)	Peas (†)	Parsnips (†)	Parsley (†)	Onions, Bunching (+)	Onions, Bulb (+)	Okra (†)	Mustard (+)	Lettuce (+)	Leeks (+)	Kohlrabi (+)	Kale (+)	Jicama (†)	Herbs (†,‡)	Endive (+)	Eggplant (†)*	Cucumbers (†)	Corn (†)	Collards (+)	Chives (+)	Celery (+)	Cauliflower (+)*	Carrots (†)	Cantaloupe (+)*	Cabbage (+)*	Brussels Sprouts (+)*	Broccoli (†)*	Beets (+)	Beans, Pole (†)	Beans, Lima (†)	Beans, Bush (†)	Asparagus (†)
JAN		•	•	•	•				•	•	•	•	•	•	•		•	•	•	•		•		•	•	•	•			•	•	•	•	•	•	•	•	•	•		•		•	•	•	•	•	•
FEB		•	•	•	•	•	•				•	•	•	•	•		•	•		•		•		•	•	•	•			•	•	•	•	•	•	•	•	•	•	•	•		•	•	•	•	•	•
MAR		•	•	•			•			•			•	•			•	•		•		•		•						•			•	•					•				•	•	•	•	
APR			•	•	•	•												•												•	•												•	•	•	•	
MAY				•	•	•	•											•											•																			
JUN					•	•																																										
JUL					•																																											
AUG	•	•									•			•									•												•	•			•						•	•		
SEP	•	•								•	•	•	•	•			•	•																	•	•			•	•	•		•	•	•	•	•	
OCT		•	•	•				•		•	•	•	•	•			•	•	•	•		•		•			•			•			•		•	•	•	•		•	•	•	•	•	•	•	•	•
NOV		•	•	•				•		•	•	•	•	•			•	•		•		•		•			•			•			•		•	•	•	•		•	•	•	•	•	•	•	•	•
DEC		•	•	•						•	•	•	•	•			•	•		•		•		•	•		•			•			•	•	•	•	•	•		•	•	•	•	•	•	•	•	•

‡ = Deep Roots † = Intermediate Root Depth + = Shallow Root Depth *Best transplanted into the garden after starting in flats or individual containers

ZONE 09

REGIONAL PLANTING CALENDAR
Brownsville, Texas; Houston, Texas; Fort Pierce, Florida; St. Augustine, Florida

Plant seeds in:	Winter Zucchini (†)	Watermelons (†)	Turnips (+)	Tomatoes (‡)*	Swiss Chard (†)	Sunflowers (†)	Squash, Winter (‡)	Squash, Summer (+)	Spinach (+)	Rutabagas (‡)	Roquette (+)	Radishes (+)	Pumpkin (‡)	Popcorn (†)	Potatoes (‡)	Peppers (‡)	Peas (†)	Parsnips (‡)	Parsley (†)	Onions, Bunching (+)	Onions, Bulb (†)	Okra (†)	Mustard (†)	Lettuce (+)	Leeks (†)	Kohlrabi (+)	Kale (†)	Jicama (‡)	Herbs (‡/†)	Endive (+)	Eggplant (†)*	Cucumbers (†)	Corn (†)	Collards (+)	Chives (+)	Celery (+)	Cauliflower (+)*	Carrots (†)	Cantaloupe (+)	Cabbage (+)*	Brussels Sprouts (+)*	Broccoli (+)*	Beets (+)	Beans, Pole (†)	Beans, Lima (†)	Beans, Bush (†)	Asparagus (†)
JAN		•							•		•	•			•			•	•		•		•				•		•					•	•					•		•	•				•
FEB			•	•	•	•			•		•	•			•	•			•		•		•				•		•											•		•	•			•	•
MAR	•	•	•	•	•	•	•	•	•	•	•	•	•	•	•	•	•		•	•	•	•	•	•	•	•	•	•	•	•	•	•						•	•	•	•	•	•	•	•	•	•
APR	•	•	•	•	•	•					•	•	•	•		•			•			•	•					•	•		•	•	•					•	•			•	•	•	•	•	
MAY	•	•		•	•	•					•	•	•	•		•			•			•						•	•		•	•	•					•	•							•	
JUN	•	•		•	•						•	•		•		•			•			•							•		•	•	•					•	•				•				
JUL	•	•		•		•					•	•		•		•			•			•									•	•	•					•	•	•							
AUG	•	•	•	•							•	•				•			•			•									•	•	•	•	•			•	•	•			•	•			
SEP	•		•		•						•	•				•	•		•	•	•	•	•	•	•	•	•		•	•	•	•	•	•	•	•	•	•	•	•	•	•	•	•		•	
OCT	•		•		•						•	•					•		•	•	•		•	•	•	•	•		•	•	•			•				•		•		•	•			•	•
NOV		•	•		•						•	•	•	•			•		•	•	•		•	•	•	•	•		•	•				•				•		•	•	•	•				•
DEC		•	•		•												•		•	•	•		•	•	•	•	•		•	•				•				•		•		•	•				

‡ = Deep Roots   † = Intermediate Root Depth   + = Shallow Root Depth   *Best transplanted into the garden after starting in flats or individual containers

REGIONAL PLANTING CALENDAR

Austin, Texas; Dallas, Texas; Gainesville, Florida; Tifton, Georgia

Columns (crops): Watermelons (‡), Turnips (+), Tomatoes (‡)*, Sweet Potato (‡), Squash, Winter (‡), Squash, Summer (‡), Spinach, New Zealand (+), Spinach (+), Shallot (+), Salsify (‡), Rutabagas (‡), Radishes (+), Potatoes (‡), Peppers (†), Peas, Black-eyed (†), Peas (†), Parsnips (‡), Onions, Bunching (+), Onions, Bulb (+), Okra (†), Mustard (†), Lettuce (+), Leeks (+), Kohlrabi (+), Kale (+), Jicama (‡), Herbs (‡,+), Garlic (+), Endive (+), Eggplant (†)*, Dandelion (‡), Cucumbers (†), Corn (†), Collards (+), Chicory (‡), Chard (†), Celery (+), Cauliflower (+)*, Carrots (‡), Cantaloupe (†), Cabbage (+)*, Broccoli (+)*, Beets (+), Beans, Lima (†), Beans, Snap (†), Asparagus (‡)

Plant seeds in:

- **JAN:** Spinach, Shallot, Radishes, Potatoes, Peas, Parsnips, Lettuce, Leeks, Garlic, Carrots, Cabbage, Asparagus
- **FEB:** Turnips, Spinach, Shallot, Salsify, Rutabagas, Radishes, Potatoes, Peas, Parsnips, Mustard, Lettuce, Leeks, Garlic, Endive, Dandelion, Chicory, Carrots, Cabbage, Broccoli, Asparagus
- **MAR:** Watermelons, Tomatoes, Squash Winter, Squash Summer, Spinach New Zealand, Radishes, Potatoes, Peppers, Peas Black-eyed, Lettuce, Leeks, Garlic, Endive, Eggplant, Cucumbers, Corn, Chicory, Cantaloupe, Cabbage, Broccoli, Beets, Beans Snap, Asparagus
- **APR:** Watermelons, Tomatoes, Sweet Potato, Squash Summer, Potatoes, Peppers, Peas Black-eyed, Mustard, Herbs, Garlic, Corn, Chicory, Cabbage, Beets, Beans Lima, Beans Snap
- **MAY:** Peas Black-eyed, Peas, Mustard, Chicory, Beans Lima, Beans Snap
- **JUN:** Tomatoes, Sweet Potato, Squash Winter, Spinach New Zealand, Salsify, Peppers, Mustard, Cucumbers, Corn, Chicory, Chard, Carrots, Cantaloupe
- **JUL:** Watermelons, Tomatoes, Spinach New Zealand, Peas Black-eyed, Peas, Mustard, Cucumbers, Corn, Collards, Celery, Carrots, Cantaloupe, Cabbage, Beans Lima, Beans Snap
- **AUG:** Turnips, Spinach New Zealand, Salsify, Rutabagas, Radishes, Potatoes, Peppers, Mustard, Cucumbers, Corn, Collards, Chicory, Chard, Celery, Cauliflower, Carrots, Cabbage, Broccoli, Beets, Beans Lima, Beans Snap
- **SEP:** Turnips, Spinach, Shallot, Salsify, Rutabagas, Radishes, Potatoes, Mustard, Lettuce, Leeks, Collards, Chicory, Chard, Beets
- **OCT:** Turnips, Spinach, Shallot, Radishes, Peas, Onions Bulb, Mustard, Dandelion, Chicory, Beets
- **NOV:** Spinach, Radishes, Peas, Mustard, Garlic
- **DEC:** Garlic, Asparagus

‡ = Deep Roots   † = Intermediate Root Depth   + = Shallow Root Depth   *Best transplanted into the garden after starting in flats or individual containers

ZONE 07

REGIONAL PLANTING CALENDAR
Oklahoma City, Oklahoma; Little Rock, Arkansas; Griffin, Georgia; South Boston, Virginia

Columns (left to right): Turnips (+)*, Tomatoes (‡)*, Swiss Chard (‡), Sweet Potatoes (‡), Sunflowers (‡), Strawberry (‡), Squash, Winter (‡), Squash, Summer (†), Spinach (+), Shallot (+), Scallion (+), Rutabagas (‡), Rhubarb (‡), Radishes (+), Pumpkin (‡), Potatoes (‡), Pigeon Peas (†), Peppers (†), Peas (†), Peanut (†), Parsnips (‡), Parsley (+), Onions, Bulb (+), Okra (‡), Mustard(+), Lettuce (+), Leeks (+), Kohlrabi (+), Kale (+), Horseradish, Herbs (‡)*, Gourds (+), Garlic (+), Fennel (+)*, Endive (+), Eggplant (†)*, Dill (‡), Cucumbers (†), Corn (‡), Collards (+), Chives (+), Chinese Cabbage (+)*, Celery (+), Cauliflower (+)*, Carrots (†), Cantaloupe (†), Cabbage (+)*, Brussels Sprouts (+)*, Broccoli Raab(+)*, Broccoli (+)*, Beets (†), Beans, Pole (†), Beans, Bush (†), Basil (+)*, Asparagus (‡)

Plant seeds in:

- **JAN** — Peas
- **FEB** — Spinach; Radishes; Potatoes; Peas; Onions, Bulb; Lettuce; Carrots; Cabbage; Beets
- **MAR** — Squash, Summer; Spinach; Radishes; Potatoes; Parsley; Onions, Bulb; Lettuce; Leeks; Cauliflower; Cabbage; Beans, Bush; Basil
- **APR** — Turnips; Tomatoes; Sweet Potatoes; Squash, Winter; Squash, Summer; Spinach; Shallot; Rutabagas; Pumpkin; Potatoes; Pigeon Peas; Peppers; Peanut; Parsnips; Parsley; Onions, Bulb; Okra; Mustard; Lettuce; Leeks; Kale; Horseradish; Herbs; Gourds; Garlic; Fennel; Endive; Eggplant; Dill; Cucumbers; Corn; Collards; Chives; Chinese Cabbage; Celery; Cauliflower; Cabbage; Beans, Pole; Beans, Bush; Basil; Asparagus
- **MAY** — Turnips; Tomatoes; Swiss Chard; Sweet Potatoes; Sunflowers; Strawberry; Squash, Winter; Squash, Summer; Spinach; Shallot; Scallion; Radishes; Pumpkin; Potatoes; Pigeon Peas; Peppers; Peanut; Parsnips; Parsley; Onions, Bulb; Okra; Mustard; Lettuce; Kohlrabi; Kale; Horseradish; Herbs; Gourds; Garlic; Fennel; Endive; Eggplant; Dill; Cucumbers; Corn; Collards; Chives; Chinese Cabbage; Celery; Carrots; Beans, Pole; Beans, Bush; Basil; Asparagus
- **JUN** — Swiss Chard; Sweet Potatoes; Squash, Winter; Squash, Summer; Radishes; Pumpkin; Pigeon Peas; Okra; Herbs; Eggplant; Dill; Beans, Pole; Beans, Bush; Basil
- **JUL** — Turnips; Tomatoes; Squash, Summer; Spinach; Mustard; Cucumbers; Corn; Chinese Cabbage; Carrots; Cantaloupe; Cabbage; Brussels Sprouts; Broccoli Raab; Broccoli; Beets; Beans, Pole; Beans, Bush; Basil
- **AUG** — Spinach; Lettuce; Leeks; Kale; Horseradish; Garlic; Endive; Brussels Sprouts; Broccoli Raab; Broccoli
- **SEP** — Spinach; Onions, Bulb; Mustard; Garlic
- **OCT** — Garlic

‡ = Deep Roots   † = Intermediate Root Depth   + = Shallow Root Depth   *Best transplanted into the garden after starting in flats or individual containers

REGIONAL PLANTING CALENDAR

Branson, Missouri; St. Louis, Missouri; McMinnville, Tennessee; Lebanon, Pennsylvania

Plant seeds in:	Watermelon (+)	Turnips (+)	Tomatoes (†)*	Swiss Chard (†)	Sweet Potatoes (‡)	Sunflowers (†)	Strawberry (‡)	Squash, Winter (‡)	Squash, Summer (‡)	Spinach (+)	Shallot (+)	Scallion (+)	Rutabagas (‡)	Rhubarb (‡)	Radishes (†)	Pumpkin (‡)	Potatoes (‡)	Peppers (†)	Peas (†)	Peanut (†)	Parsnips (‡)	Parsley (†)	Onions, Bulb (†)	Okra (†)	Mustard (+)	Lettuce (+)	Leeks (+)	Kohlrabi (+)	Kale (+)	Horseradish (†)	Herbs (‡,+)	Gourds (†)	Garlic (+)	Fennel (+)*	Endive (+)	Eggplant (†)*	Dill (‡)	Cucumbers (†)	Corn (‡)	Collards (+)	Chives (+)	Chinese Cabbage (+)*	Celery (‡)	Cauliflower (+)*	Carrots (†)	Cabbage (‡)*	Brussels Sprouts (+)*	Broccoli (+)*	Beets (+)	Beans, Pole (†)	Beans, Bush (†)	Basil (+)*	Asparagus (‡)
JAN																																																					
FEB																																																					
MAR		•	•							•					•	•	•		•			•	•			•	•		•							•					•		•		•	•	•	•					•
APR	•	•	•		•	•												•						•														•	•	•			•		•				•	•	•	•	•
MAY	•	•	•	•	•	•	•	•	•	•	•	•	•	•	•	•	•	•	•	•	•	•	•	•	•	•	•	•	•																				•	•	•	•	•
JUN				•	•				•	•			•		•											•						•	•					•		•	•								•	•	•	•	
JUL																																						•		•	•	•											•
AUG		•																							•	•			•									•		•	•								•	•	•	•	
SEP																																	•																				
OCT																																	•																				
NOV																																																					
DEC																																																					

‡ = Deep Roots † = Intermediate Root Depth + = Shallow Root Depth *Best transplanted into the garden after starting in flats or individual containers

REGIONAL PLANTING CALENDAR
Columbia, Missouri; Des Moines, Iowa; Chicago, Illinois; Mansfield, Pennsylvania

Crop	JAN	FEB	MAR	APR	MAY	JUN	JUL	AUG	SEP	OCT	NOV	DEC
Turnips (+)				•	•	•		•				
Tomatoes (‡)*					•	•	•					
Swiss Chard (‡)					•	•						
Sweet Potato (‡)					•	•						
Sunflower (‡)					•	•						
Strawberry (+)					•	•						
Squash, Winter (‡)					•	•						
Squash, Summer (‡)					•	•						
Spinach (+)				•	•	•						
Shallot (+)				•	•	•						
Scallion (+)				•	•	•						
Rutabagas (‡)					•	•						
Rhubarb (‡)					•	•						
Radishes (+)				•	•	•		•				
Pumpkin (‡)					•	•						
Potatoes (‡)					•	•						
Pigeon Peas (‡)					•	•						
Peppers (‡)					•							
Peas (+)				•	•							
Peanut (‡)					•							
Parsnips (‡)					•							
Parsley (+)				•	•							
Onions, Bulb (+)				•	•	•						
Okra (‡)					•	•						
Mustard (+)				•	•		•	•				
Lettuce (+)				•	•			•				
Leeks (+)				•	•							
Kohlrabi (+)					•							
Kale (‡)					•							
Horseradish (‡)					•							
Herbs (‡,†)				•	•							
Gourds (‡)				•	•	•						
Garlic (+)*					•				•	•		
Fennel (+)*				•	•							
Endive (+)					•							
Eggplant (‡)*					•							
Dill (‡)					•	•	•					
Cucumbers (‡)				•	•	•						
Corn (‡)					•	•						
Collards (‡)					•		•	•				
Chives (+)					•		•					
Chinese Cabbage (+)*				•	•		•	•				
Celery (+)*				•	•		•					
Cauliflower (+)*				•	•		•	•				
Carrots (‡)				•	•							
Cabbage (+)*				•	•							
Brussels Sprouts (+)*					•		•	•				
Broccoli Raab (+)*					•		•	•				
Broccoli (+)*				•	•		•	•				
Beets (‡)					•	•	•	•				
Beans, Pole (‡)					•	•						
Beans, Bush (‡)					•	•	•	•				
Basil (†)*					•	•	•	•				
Asparagus (‡)				•	•							

‡ = Deep Roots   † = Intermediate Root Depth   + = Shallow Root Depth   *Best transplanted into the garden after starting in flats or individual containers

REGIONAL PLANTING CALENDAR

Lewistown, Montana; Casper, Wyoming; Northwood, Iowa; Minneapolis/St.Paul, Minnesota

Plant seeds in:

Crop	JAN	FEB	MAR	APR	MAY	JUN	JUL	AUG	SEP	OCT	NOV	DEC
Watermelons (‡)					●	●						
Turnips (†)				●		●		●				
Tomatoes (‡)*					●	●						
Swiss Chard (†)					●	●						
Sweet Potato (‡)					●	●						
Squash, Winter (‡)					●	●						
Squash, Summer (†)					●	●						
Spinach (+)				●	●	●		●				
Rutabagas (‡)					●	●						
Rhubarb (‡)					●	●						
Radishes (+)				●	●	●		●				
Pumpkins				●		●						
Potatoes (‡)					●	●						
Peppers (†)					●	●						
Peas (†)				●	●	●						
Parsnips (‡)					●	●						
Parsley (†)				●	●	●						
Onions, sets (+)				●	●	●						
Onions, seeds (+)				●	●							
Okra (†)						●						
Muskmelon						●						
Lettuce (+)				●	●	●	●	●				
Kohlrabi (+)						●		●				
Kale (+)				●	●	●						
Horseradish (†)					●	●						
Herbs (‡,†)						●						
Garlic (+)				●						●	●	
Endive (+)						●						
Eggplant (†)*						●						
Cucumbers (†)					●	●						
Corn (‡)				●	●	●						
Collards (+)					●	●	●					
Celery (+)				●	●	●						
Cauliflower (+)*				●	●	●						
Carrots (†)				●	●	●						
Cabbage, Chinese (+)*				●			●					
Cabbage, Late (+)*					●	●						
Cabbage, Early (+)*				●	●							
Brussels Sprouts (+)*				●								
Broccoli (+)*				●	●							
Beets (+)					●	●	●					
Beans, Lima (†)					●	●						
Beans, Dry (†)					●	●						
Beans, Pole (†)					●	●	●					
Beans, Bush (†)					●	●	●					
Asparagus (‡)				●	●	●						

‡ = Deep Roots   † = Intermediate Root Depth   + = Shallow Root Depth   *Best transplanted into the garden after starting in flats or individual containers

ZONE 03

REGIONAL PLANTING CALENDAR
Sidney, Montana; International Falls, Minnesota; Tomahawk, Wisconsin

Zucchini (‡)	Turnips (+)	Tomatoes (‡)*	Swiss Chard (†)	Squash, Winter (‡)	Squash, Summer (‡)	Spinach (+)	Radishes (+)	Pumpkin (‡)	Potatoes (†)	Peppers (‡)	Peas (†)	Parsnips (†)	Parsley (†)	Onions, seeds (+)	Onions, sets (+)	Leeks (+)	Lettuce (+)	Kale (±,†)	Herbs (±,†)	Garlic (+)	Eggplant (†)*	Cucumbers (†)	Corn (‡)	Chives (+)	Celery (+)	Cauliflower (+)*	Carrots (†)	Cabbage, Chinese (+)*	Cabbage, Late (+)*	Cabbage, Early (+)*	Brussels Sprouts (+)*	Broccoli (+)*	Beets (†)	Beans, Lima (†)	Beans, Dry (†)	Beans, Pole (†)	Beans, Bush (†)	Basil (†)*	Arugula (+)	Artichokes (†)	Plant seeds in:
																																									JAN
																																									FEB
																•								•	•	•														•	MAR
			•	•	•			•			•		•		•	•	•	•				•		•	•	•				•	•	•							•	•	APR
•	•	•	•	•	•	•	•				•	•		•		•		•		•		•	•	•	•	•					•		•	•	•	•	•	•	•		MAY
•	•					•	•				•	•						•	•									•	•				•	•					•		JUN
																																									JUL
																																									AUG
																																									SEP
																																									OCT
																																									NOV
																																									DEC

‡ = Deep Roots   † = Intermediate Root Depth   + = Shallow Root Depth   *Best transplanted into the garden after starting in flats or individual containers

FOOD FOR THOUGHT AND ACTION

STATISTICS

Between 1935 and 1997 the total number of farms in the United States decreased from approximately 6.3 million to 2.1 million. The average farm increased from 147 acres to 461 acres.

> – Robert A. Hoppe and Penni Korb, "Large and Small Farms: Trends and Characteristics, Structural and Financial Characteristics of U.S. Farms," *Agriculture Information Bulletin* 797, U.S. Dept. of Agriculture, March 2005

Every minute of every day America loses 2 acres of farmland. Between 1982 and 1997 the U.S. population grew 17 percent, while the amount of land that is urbanized grew 47 percent.

> – American Farmland Trust, 2007, www.farmland.org

Lawns cover 30 million acres of the United States.

> – Virginia Scott Jenkins, *The Lawn: A History of an American Obsession*, Smithsonian Books, 1994

Americans spend $750 million a year on grass seed alone and more than $25 billion on do-it-yourself lawn and garden care.

> – Diana Balmori, F. Herbert Bormann, and Gordon T. Geballe, *Redesigning the American Lawn: A Search for Environmental Harmony*, Yale University Press, 2001 (2nd rev. ed.)

Lawns use more equipment, labor, fuel, and agricultural toxins than industrial farming, making lawns the largest agricultural sector in the United States.

> – Richard Burdick, "The Biology of Lawns," *Discover*, July 2003

Approximately 9 percent of some types of air pollutants nationwide come from the small engines on lawn and garden equipment. In metropolitan areas the concentration of lawns causes this figure to increase to 33 percent.

> – Roger Westerholm, "Measurement of Regulated and Unregulated Exhaust Emissions from a Lawn Mower with and without an Oxidizing Catalyst," *Journal of Environmental Science and Technology* 35, June 1, 2001

The lawns in the United States consume around 270 billion gallons of water per week—enough to water 81 million acres of organic vegetables all summer long. An average-size lawn of around a third of an acre could, while maintaining a small area for recreation, produce enough vegetables to feed a family of 6.

> – Heather C. Flores, *Food Not Lawns: How to Turn Your Yard into a Garden and Your Neighborhood into a Community*, Chelsea Green, 2006

Of 30 commonly used lawn pesticides, 13 are probable carcinogens, 14 are linked with birth defects, 18 with reproductive effects, 20 with liver or kidney damage, 18 with neurotoxicity, and 28 are irritants.

– National Coalition for Pesticide-Free Lawns, 2005, www.beyondpesticides.org/pesticidefreelawns

Homeowners use up to 10 times more chemical pesticides per acre on their lawns than farmers use on crops.

– "News Release: What's Happening to the Frogs," U.S. Fish and Wildlife Service website, July 6, 2000, www.fws.gov/contaminants/ Issues/Amphibians.cfm

Between 1985 and 2000 the price of fresh fruit and vegetables Americans consumed increased almost 40 percent.

– Judy Putnam, Jane Allshouse, and Linda Scott Kantor, "Weighing In on Obesity," *FoodReview* 25:3, United States Dept. of Agriculture, 2003

In 1999 the food system was estimated to account for 16 percent of total U.S. energy consumption.

– *Inventory of Greenhouse Gas Emissions and Sinks 1990–1999*, Environmental Protection Agency, 1999

The typical American meal contains, on average, ingredients from at least 5 countries outside of the United States. The produce in the average American dinner is trucked 1,500 miles to reach our plates, up 22 percent in the past 2 decades.

– Rich Pirog, "Checking the Food Odometer: Comparing Food Miles for Local versus Conventional Produce Sales to Iowa Institutions," Leopold Center for Sustainable Agriculture, July 2003, www. leopold.iastate.edu/pubs/staff/files/food_travel072103.pdf

Thirty-nine percent of fruit and 12 percent of vegetables eaten by Americans are produced in other countries.

– World Resources Institute, IUCN-The World Conservation Union, United Nations Environment Program (UNEP), *Global Biodiversity Strategy: Guidelines for Action to Save, Study and Use Earth's Biotic Wealth Sustainably and Equitably*, World Resources Institute, 1992

Locally grown produce travels an average of 56 miles from farm to packaging distribution center to grocery store to dinner table. Six to 12 percent of every dollar spent on food consumed in the home comes from transportation costs.

– V. James Rhodes, *The Agricultural Marketing System*, Gorsuch, Scarisbrick, 1993 (4th ed.)

One to 2 percent of America's food is locally grown.

– Estimate by Brian Halweil, Worldwatch Institute, reported by Jim Robbins, "Think Global, Eat Local," *Los Angeles Times Magazine*, July 31, 2005

Although 5,000 different species of plants have been used as food by humans, the majority of the world's population is now fed by less than 20 plant species.

– Dept. of the Environment, Sport and Territories, "Biodiversity and Its Value," Biodiversity Series, paper no. 1, Dept. of the Environment, Sport, and Territories of the Commonwealth of Australia, 1993

Almost 96 percent of the commercial vegetable varieties available in 1903 are now extinct.

– Center for Biodiversity and Conservation, "Biodiversity and Your Food: Did You Know?" American Museum of Natural History, research.amnh.org/biodiversity/center/living/Food/index.html

RESOURCES

Cooperative Extension Service

The Cooperative Extension Service is an invaluable resource for all gardeners. Provided by each state's designated land-grant university, the Co-op Extension offers master gardener training, soil testing, and information on pests, diseases, and plants particular to the gardener's region. USDA Cooperative State Research, Education, and Extension 202.720.7441 www.csrees.usda.gov/Extension

Gardening Information

CORNELL HOME GARDENING
www.gardening.cornell.edu/homegardening
General gardening techniques and common vegetable growing guides

NATIONAL GARDENING ASSOCIATION
1100 Dorset St.
South Burlington, Vt. 05403
802.863.5251 www.garden.org
General gardening information and events

U.S. ENVIRONMENTAL PROTECTION AGENCY GREENSCAPES PROGRAM
Office of Solid Waste
1200 Pennsylvania Ave. N.W.
Washington, D.C. 20460
www.epa.gov/epaoswer/non-hw/green/owners.htm
Techniques to minimize the resources required by gardens

Online Gardening Databases and Forums

Online databases and forums provide direct answers to the gardener's questions from either horticulturists or a community of gardeners.

GARDENWEB FORUM
www.gardenweb.com

PLANTFACTS
plantfacts.osu.edu

PLANTS FOR A FUTURE
www.pfaf.org

PLANT*TALK*
www.ext.colostate.edu/ptlk

VEGETABLE RESEARCH AND INFORMATION CENTER
vric.ucdavis.edu

Organic, Biodynamics, and Permaculture Resources

BIODYNAMIC FARMING AND GARDENING ASSOCIATION
25844 Butler Rd.
Junction City, Ore. 97448
888.516.7797 www. biodynamics.com
Information on biodynamic gardening and a planting calendar based on the moon cycles

PERMACULTURE INSTITUTE
Box 3702, Santa Fe, N.M. 87501
505.455.0514 www.permaculture.org
Network of permaculture groups and information on training workshops

RODALE INSTITUTE–NEW FARM
611 Siegriedale Rd.
Kutztown, Penn. 19530
610.683.1400 www.rodaleinstitute.org, www.newfarm.org
General resource for organic gardening

Research and Organizations

AMERICAN FARMLAND TRUST
1200 18th St. N.W., suite 800
Washington, D.C. 20036
202.331.7300 www.farmland.org

BIONEERS
6 Cerro Cir.
Lamy, N.M. 87540
877.246.6337 www.bioneers.org

THE ECOLOGICAL FARMING ASSOCIATION
406 Main St., suite 313
Watsonville, Calif. 95076
831.763.2111 www.eco-farm.org

FOOD ROUTES
Box 55, Arnot, Penn. 16911
570.638.3608 www.foodroutes.org

THE LAND INSTITUTE
2440 E. Water Well Rd.
Salina, Kan. 67401
785.823.5376 www.landinstitute.org

NATIONAL SUSTAINABLE AGRICULTURE INFORMATION SERVICE
Box 3657, Fayetteville, Ark. 72702
www.attra.org

Seed Resources

BAY AREA SEED INTERCHANGE LIBRARY [BASIL]
2530 San Pablo Ave.
Berkeley, Calif. 94702
www.ecologycenter.org/basil

ORGANIC SEED ALLIANCE
Box 772, Port Townsend, Wash. 98368
360.385.7192 www.seedalliance.org

SAVING OUR SEED
286 Dixie Hollow
Louisa, Va. 23093
540.894.8865 www.savingourseed.org

SOUTHERN SEED LEGACY
Dept. of Anthropology
University of Georgia
250A Baldwin Hall
Jackson St.
Athens, Ga. 30602
706.542.1430 www.uga.edu/ebl/ssl/

Soil Testing

SOIL FOODWEB, INC.
728 S.W. Wake Robin Ave.
Corvallis, Ore. 97333
541.752.5066
and
555 Hallock Ave., suite 7
Port Jefferson Station, N.Y. 11776
631.474.8848 www.soilfoodweb.com
Tests soil samples for harmful pollutants and beneficial microorganisms

BIBLIOGRAPHY

Stephen Albert, *The Kitchen Garden Grower's Guide: A Practical Vegetable and Herb Garden Encyclopedia*, BookSurge, 2008

Liberty Hyde Bailey, *Garden-Making: Suggestions for the Utilizing of Home Grounds*, 1898; reprint, Obscure Press, 2009

Jeff Ball, *The Self-Sufficient Suburban Garden*, Rodale, 1984

Mel Bartholomew, *Square Foot Gardening*, Rodale, 1981

Fern Marchall Bradley and Barbara W. Ellis, eds., *Rodale's All-New Encyclopedia of Organic Gardening: The Indispensable Resource for Every Gardener*, Rodale, 1992 (2nd rev. ed.)

Norris Brenzel, *Sunset: Western Garden*, Sunset Books, 2001 (7th ed., rev. and updated)

Rita Buchanan, *The Shaker Herb and Garden Book*, Houghton Mifflin, 1996

Eliot Coleman, *The New Organic Grower: A Master's Manual of Tools and Techniques for the Home and Market Gardener,* Chelsea Green, 1995 (2nd ed., rev. and expanded)

François Couplan, *Encyclopedia of Edible Plants of North America*, Keats, 1998

Rosalind Creasy, *Edible Landscaping*, Sierra Club Books, 2010

Tanya L. K. Denckla, *The Gardener's A–Z Guide to Growing Organic Food*, Storey, 2004 (rev. ed.)

Heather C. Flores, *Food Not Lawns: How to Turn Your Yard into a Garden and Your Neighborhood into a Community*, Chelsea Green, 2006

Fred Hagy, *Landscaping with Fruits and Vegetables*, Overlook, 2001

John Jeavons, *How to Grow More Vegetables (and Fruits, Nuts, Berries, Grains, and Other Crops) Than You Ever Thought Possible on Less Land Than You Can Imagine*, Ten Speed Press, 2006 (7th ed.)

Kelly Kindscher, *Edible Wild Plants of the Prairie*, University Press of Kansas, 1987

Donald R. Kirk, *Wild Edible Plants of Western North America,* Naturegraph, 1970

Robert Kourik, *Designing and Maintaining Your Edible Landscape Naturally*, Permanent, 2005

Joy Larkom, *Grow Your Own Vegetables*, Frances Lincoln, 2002 (rev. ed.)

Stella Otto, *The Backyard Orchardist: A Complete Guide to Growing Fruit Trees in the Home Garden*, Chelsea Green, 1995 (2nd rev. ed.)

Lee Reich, *Uncommon Fruits for Every Garden*, Timber Press, 2004 (2nd ed.)

Jan Riggenbach, *Midwest Gardener's Handbook: The What, Where, When, How, and Why of Gardening in the Midwest*, Cool Springs Press, 1999

F. F. Rockwell, *Home Vegetable Gardening: A Complete and Practical Guide to the Planting and Care of All Vegetables, Fruits, and Berries Worth Growing for Home Use*, 1911; reprint, Forgotten Books, 2008

R. J. Ruppenthal, *Fresh Food from Small Spaces: The Square-Inch Gardener's Guide to Year-Round Growing, Fermenting, and Sprouting*, Chelsea Green, 2008

John Seymour, *New Complete Self-Sufficiency*, Dorling Kindersley, 2003 (rev. ed.)

Rachel Snyder, *Gardening in the Heartland*, University Press of Kansas, 1992

Steve Solomon, *Gardening When It Counts: Growing Food in Hard Times*, New Society Publishers, 2006

Ruth Stout, *The Ruth Stout No-Work Garden Book*, Bantam, 1971

Muriel Sweet, *Common Edible and Useful Plants of the West*, Naturegraph, 1976

Frances Tenenbaum, ed., *Taylor's Master Guide to Gardening*, Houghton Mifflin, 2001

Roger Vick, *Gardening: Plains and Upper Midwest*, Fulcrum, 1991

Pat Welsh, *Pat Welsh's Southern California Gardening: A Month-by-Month Guide*, Chronicle, 1999

Biodynamic Gardening and Permaculture

Graham Bell, *The Permaculture Garden*, Chelsea Green, 2008

Toby Hemenway, *Gaia's Garden: A Guide to Home-Scale Permaculture*, Chelsea Green, 2001

David Holmgren, *Permaculture: Principles and Pathways beyond Sustainability*, Holmgren Design Services, 2002

Bill Mollison and Reny Mia Slay, *Permaculture: A Designers' Manual*, Tagari, 1997

Wolf D. Storl, *Culture and Horticulture: A Philosophy of Gardening*, Biodynamic Literature, 1979

Patrick Whitefield, *How to Make a Forest Garden*, Permanent, 2002

Companion Planting and Seed Saving

Suzanne Ashworth and Kent Whealy, *Seed to Seed: Seed Saving and Growing Techniques for Vegetable Gardeners*, Seed Savers Exchange, 2002 (2nd ed.)

Sally Jean Cunningham, *Great Garden Companions: A Companion-Planting System for a Beautiful, Chemical-Free Vegetable Garden*, Rodale, 2000

Carol Deppe, *Breed Your Own Vegetable Varieties: The Gardener's and Farmer's Guide to Plant Breeding and Seed Saving*, Chelsea Green, 2000 (2nd rev. ed.)

Louise Riotte, *Carrots Love Tomatoes: Secrets of Companion Planting for Successful Gardening*, Storey, 1998 (2nd ed.)

Composting, Pruning, Pest Control, and Rainwater Harvesting

Mary Appelhof, *Worms Eat My Garbage: How to Set Up and Maintain a Worm Composting System*, Flower Press, 1997

Suzy Banks and Richard Heinichen, *Rainwater Collection for the Mechanically Challenged*, Tank Town, 2006

Steve Bradley, *The Pruner's Bible: A Step-by-Step Guide to Pruning Every Plant in Your Garden*, Rodale, 2005

Barbara W. Ellis and Fern Marchall Bradley, eds., *The Organic Gardener's Handbook of Natural Insect and Disease Control: A Complete Problem-Solving Guide to Keeping Your Garden and Yard Healthy without Chemicals*, Rodale, 1996

Brad Lancaster, *Rainwater Harvesting for Drylands: Guiding Principles to Welcome Rain into Your Life and Landscape*, Chelsea Green, 2006

Art Ludwig, *Create an Oasis with Greywater: Choosing, Building, and Using Greywater Systems—Includes Branched Drains*, Oasis Design, 2006 (5th rev. ed.)

Deborah L. Martin, *The Rodale Book of Composting*, Rodale, 1999 (rev. ed.)

Allan Shepherd, *How to Make Soil and Save Earth*, Centre for Alternative Technology, 2003

Kenneth Thompson, *Compost: The Natural Way to Make Food for Your Garden*, Dorling Kindersley, 2007

Food, Plants, and Ecology

Steven B. Carroll and Steven D. Salt, *Ecology for Gardeners*, Timber Press, 2004

Dorothy Crispo, *The Story of Our Fruits and Vegetables*, Devin-Adair, 1968

Wes Jackson, *Becoming Native to This Place*, Counterpoint, 1994

Wes Jackson and William Vitek, *Rooted in the Land*, Yale University Press, 1996

Sandor Ellix Katz, *The Revolutions Will Not Be Microwaved: Inside America's Underground Food Movements*, Chelsea Green, 2006

Sue Leaf, *Potato City: Nature, History, and Community in the Age of Sprawl*, Borealis, 2004

Katherine Lerza and Michael Jacobson, *Food for People Not Profit: A Sourcebook on the Food Crisis*, Ballantine, 1975

Marion Nestle, *Food Politics: How the Food Industry Influences Nutrition and Health*, University of California Press, 2003

Michael Pollan, *The Botany of Desire: A Plant's-Eye View of the World*, Random House, 2001

————, *The Omnivore's Dilemma: A Natural History of Four Meals*, Penguin, 2006

William Woys Weaver, *100 Vegetables and Where They Came From*, Algonquin, 2000

The History of the Lawn

Diana Balmori, F. Herbert Bormann, and Gordon T. Geballe, *Redesigning the American Lawn: A Search for Environmental Harmony*, Yale University Press, 2001 (2nd rev. ed.)

Ted Steinberg, *American Green: The Obsessive Quest for the Perfect Lawn*, W. W. Norton, 2006

Georges Teyssot, ed., *The American Lawn*, Princeton Architectural Press, 1999

Urban Agriculture and Homesteading

John E. Bryan, *Small World Vegetable Gardening*, 101 Productions, 1977

Mary Lee Coe, *Growing with Community Gardening*, Countryman Press, 1978

Kelly Coyne and Erik Knutzen, *The Urban Homestead: Your Guide to Self-Sufficient Living in the Heart of the City*, Process, 2008

Abigail R. Gehring, ed., *Homesteading: A Back-to-Basics Guide to Growing Your Own Food, Canning, Keeping Chickens, Generating Your Own Energy, Crafting, Herbal Medicine, and More*, Skyhorse, 2009

Laura J. Lawson, *City Bountiful: A Century of Community Gardening in America*, University of California Press, 2005

Carleen Madigan, *The Backyard Homestead*, Storey, 2009

Margaret Morton and Diana Balmori, *Transitory Gardens, Uprooted Lives*, Yale University Press, 1995

Susan Naimark, ed., *A Handbook of Community Gardening*, Charles Scribner's Sons, 1982

Richard Reynolds, *On Guerrilla Gardening: The Why, What, and How of Cultivating Neglected Public Space*, Bloomsbury, 2008

David Tracey, *Guerrilla Gardening: A Manualfesto*, New Society, 2007

Andre Viljoen, ed., *Continuous Productive Urban Landscapes: Designing Agriculture for Sustainable Cities*, Architectural Press, 2005

Piers Warren, *How to Store Your Garden Produce: The Key to Self-Sufficiency*, Green Books, 2003

Harry Wiland and Dale Bell, *Edens Lost and Found: How Ordinary Citizens Are Restoring Our Great American Cities*, Chelsea Green, 2006

Peter Lamborn Wilson and Bill Weinberg, eds., *Avant Gardening: Ecological Struggle in the City and the World*, Autonomedia, 1999

Victory Gardens, Monticello, and the History of Home Edible Gardening

Amy Bentley, *Eating for Victory: Food Rationing and the Politics of Domesticity*, University of Illinois Press, 1998

Susan Campbell, *A History of Kitchen Gardening*, Frances Lincoln, 2005

Peter J. Hatch, ed., *Thomas Jefferson's Garden Book*, University of North Carolina Press, 2001 (2nd ed.)

Angelo M. Pellegrini, *The Unprejudiced Palate: Classic Thoughts on Food and the Good Life*, Modern Library, 2005

Michael Pollan, *Second Nature: A Gardener's Education*, Atlantic Monthly Press, 1991

Victory Garden Guide (pamphlet), U.S. Dept. of Agriculture, 1948

ABOUT THE CONTRIBUTORS

Fritz Haeg works between his occasional architecture and design practice, Fritz Haeg Studio; the happenings and gatherings of Sundown Salon; the ecology initiatives of Gardenlab, which include Edible Estates; and his role as an educator. His ongoing Animal Estates initiative proposes the strategic reintroduction of native animals into our cities with a series of regional events, publications, exhibitions, and design proposals. It debuted at the 2008 Whitney Biennial, with later editions produced in six cities across the U.S. and Europe. In 2006 Haeg initiated Sundown Schoolhouse, an alternative educational environment based in his geodesic dome in Los Angeles. He has taught in architecture, design, and fine art programs at CalArts, Art Center College of Design, Parsons, and the University of Southern California. He has produced projects and exhibited work at the Tate Modern; the Whitney Museum of American Art; Mass MoCA; the Institute of Contemporary Art, Philadelphia; the CCA Wattis Institute for Contemporary Arts; the Netherlands Architecture Institute, Maastricht; SFMOMA; and the MAK Center, Los Angeles, among other organizations. www.fritzhaeg.com

Essayists

Will Allen is the founder and CEO of Growing Power, an urban farm and community food center in Milwaukee. The son of a South Carolina sharecropper, Will became the first African-American to win a basketball scholarship at the University of Miami, and he went on to play as a professional in the American Basketball Association and for Belgium in the European League. After his playing days he pursued a successful business career in corporate marketing. Since his return to farming he has built Growing Power into a preeminent national training center in the methods of urban and community-based agriculture. In 2008 he was chosen as a MacArthur Fellow.

Diana Balmori's work in landscape architecture and urban design grew out of her interest in the way public space is used and designed and its role in the larger environment. Her firm, Balmori Associates, is acknowledged internationally for realizing complex urban projects that integrate sustainable systems within innovative design solutions. BALMORILABS is a branch of Dr. Balmori's studio that explores the ways in which landscape can intersect with architecture, art, and engineering. Dr. Balmori's most recent book is *The Land and Natural Development (LAND) Code: Guidelines for Sustainable Land Development* (2007). www.balmori.com

Rosalind Creasy is a garden and food writer, photographer, and landscape designer with a passion for beautiful vegetables and ecologically sensitive gardening. Her first book, *The Complete Book of Edible Landscaping* (1982), helped popularize the term "edible landscaping," now a part of the American vocabulary. *Cooking from the Garden* (1988) introduced the American public to a vast new palette of vegetables, including the then-unknown heirloom tomatoes and melons, mesclun salad greens, and blue potatoes and corn. Frustrated by America's love of lawns, for the last two decades Creasy has used her front garden to showcase an ever changing array of edibles, from hot pink amaranth to golden zucchini. Photographs of her garden and harvested edibles enrich her many lectures and writings.

Michael Pollan is the author, most recently, of *In Defense of Food: An Eater's Manifesto* (2008). His previous book, *The Omnivore's Dilemma: A Natural History of Four Meals*, was named one of the ten best books of 2006 by both the *New York Times* and the *Washington Post*. A contributing writer to the *New York Times Magazine*, Pollan is the recipient of numerous journalistic accolades, including the 2003 James Beard Award for best magazine series and the Reuters-IUCN 2000 Global Award for Environmental Journalism. Pollan is the Knight Professor of Science and Environmental Journalism at the University of California, Berkeley. www.michaelpollan.com

Eric W. Sanderson is a senior conservation ecologist at the Wildlife Conservation Society. He is an expert on species conservation planning and has contributed to efforts to save lions, tigers, Asian bears, jaguars, and other animals, and has engaged in landscape planning conservation projects worldwide. His work has been featured in the *New York Times*, *National Geographic* magazine, and the *New Yorker* and on national radio. Dr. Sanderson is the director of the Mannahatta Project, an effort to reconstruct the original ecology of Manhattan Island at the time of European discovery in the seventeenth century. In 2009 he published *Mannahatta: A Natural History of New York City* and curated an exhibition and guided the creation of a website based on the Mannahatta Project.

Lesley Stern was born in Zimbabwe, has lived in Britain and Australia, and is now professor of visual arts at the University of California, San Diego. She has published two highly acclaimed books, *The Scorsese Connection* (1995) and *The Smoking Book* (1999). She is currently completing a manuscript entitled "Gardening in a Strange Land."

Estate Owners

Brookwood House, located at the intersection of Webber and Lancaster Streets, is a block of twenty-four flats managed by Southwark Council in London, England. The residents include a mix of young families, retirees, working people, job-seekers, and people with long-term illnesses. Among the diverse residents, many languages are spoken and cultures represented. Residents from the neighboring Albury and Clandon Houses, as well as people from nearby blocks, have also become involved as gardeners at the London Edible Estate.

Michelle Christman's joyful relationship with food stems from her childhood in Pennsylvania farm country. Food continued to inspire her life when she married Chris Wei, a chef. When he retired from professional cooking to pursue a career in music, Michelle picked up her knives, left her job in pharmaceutical advertising, and launched her professional food career as the owner of ChowBaby, a company that produces organic food for babies, toddlers, and kids. The birth of their son, Atticus Huckleberry Wei, motivated them to do more for their family, their community, and their planet.

Stan Cox has worked as a senior scientist at the Land Institute in Salina, Kansas, since 2000. He held a position as a wheat geneticist with the U.S. Department of Agriculture from 1984 to 1996. In 1996 he moved to India, where he had done his dissertation research fifteen years earlier. He and his wife, Priti, moved to Salina in 2000. In addition to research in perennial grain breeding, he writes on environmental issues. His op-ed columns have appeared in the *San Jose Mercury News*, the *Denver Post*, the *Kansas City Star*, and other newspapers. He writes articles for the websites AlterNet, CounterPunch, and Common Dreams, and is the author of *Sick Planet: Corporate Food and Medicine* (2008).

Michael Foti lives in Lakewood, California, with his wife, Jennifer, and their daughters, Cecilia and June. By day he works as a software engineer; he was initially attracted to gardening as a way to unwind and relax in the outdoors after many hours in front of a computer screen. Before creating his front-yard Edible Estate he established a backyard vegetable garden and henhouse with his daughters. Michael considers himself to be a novice gardener whose efforts are proof that anyone with a modicum of dedication can grow his or her own food and take an active part in the creation and maintenance of a more humane environment.

Hudson Guild has been addressing the needs of the Chelsea community of Manhattan for more than 110 years. This multiservice settlement house provides day care, senior services, morning and evening recreation, and classes ranging from the pre-kindergarten to GED levels to more than 14,000 people each year. The population the Guild primarily serves resides in two New York City Housing Authority developments: the Robert Fulton Houses and Elliott-Chelsea Houses, where the garden is located and which is home to more than 2,000 residents.

Clarence Ridgley lives in the Liberty Heights neighborhood of Baltimore with his wife, Rudine, and works as a manufacturing supervisor. He had been mowing his front lawn for twenty-two years before the planting of his Edible Estate garden in 2008. He has four children, six grandchildren, and lots of new friends in the neighborhood who share in his garden as they walk by.

Sierra Ridge Apartments were built in 1970 and acquired by Foundation Communities in 1991. About 350 people, one-third of them children, live in 148 units in four two-story buildings. Most residents are employed in service industries or construction. Sierra Ridge is one of the most successful of Foundation Communities's eight affordable-housing properties in Austin, with a consistently high occupancy rate and a tight-knit community. The complex also features a learning center that offers after-school activities for children and classes in English and computer use. Residents who leave the community most often do so to buy houses of their own.

Photographers

The Canary Project, founded by Susannah Sayler and Edward Morris, produces visual media and artwork that deepen public understanding of climate change and energize commitment to solutions. Its work has been shown in diverse venues including science and art museums, public art installations, classrooms, the sides of buses, and city halls. Canary Project team member Curtis Hamilton photographed the Maplewood Edible Estate. www.canary-project.org

Leslie Furlong is a photographer and video artist who lives in Baltimore, Maryland. Her work explores the subject of our ever transforming landscape. She also has participated in making documentary films about social justice. Her love of plants and her interests in urban gardening, land use, and ecology led her to photograph the Edible Estates garden in Baltimore. www.lesliefurlong.com

Oto Gillen is based in New York City, where he participates in a broad range of projects that include photography, filmmaking, collaborative public art interventions, and music composition and performance. He has taken part in a number of group shows and his work has been published through Creative Time and in *Vice* and *V* magazines. He is working on a photography book entitled *New York, New York*.

Sunshine Mathon works in Austin as the design and development director at Foundation Communities, overseeing the design and construction of new affordable-housing communities in central Texas. He also directs a summer camp for boys in Vermont and travels extensively throughout the world. In all aspects of his work and play, photography provides a pervasive medium for exploration and sharing with others.

Taidgh O'Neill is an artist based in Los Angeles. His work explores the relationship between humans and their immediate and global environments. O'Neill uses photography to catalogue people's durational occupation of space, land movement and development, energy usage, gardening, landscaping, and city planning. His interest in the Edible Estates garden in Lakewood stemmed from his desire to document examples of productive change.

Heiko Prigge lived and worked in Cape Town and Miami before moving to London, where he photographed the Edible Estates garden. He shoots for the *New York Times* and the U.K. editions of *The Face, Wallpaper, Esquire, GQ,* and other publications. His exhibitions have included *One Moment Please* at the Victoria and Albert Museum (1999) and, with artist Alexandra Mir, *State of Play* at the Serpentine Gallery, London (2004).

ILLUSTRATION LIST AND CREDITS

Courtesy of Arthouse, 106, 112, 113 **Matt Au,** 62, 72, 90, 98 **Lisa Anne Auerbach,** 144, 146 **Meghan Barrier,** 143 **Christopher Brandow,** 147 **Justin Bursch,** 149 **Annie Tiberio Cameron,** 155 **City of Lakewood,** 71 left, Lakewood; 71 right, an original Lakewood house **Dale Cole,** 69 **Barbara Cooper,** 154 **Stan Cox,** 68 center and right **Rosalind Creasy,** Creasy house: 49, with front lawn removed; 51, children harvesting pumpkins; 52, front garden **Courtesy of Descanso Gardens,** 131 bottom three, 132 bottom center, 133 bottom left and bottom right **Chris Edwards,** 152 **Leslie Furlong,** front cover, front flap (left, third down), 114, 115 right, 117–21, 123 bottom four, 124, 125 **Oto Gillen,** front flap (top left), 58 far left, 135 right, 138–41, 142 left and center, back flap (author photo) **Courtesy of Growing Power,** 28–35 **Fritz Haeg** (top right; left, second down); 9, White House, Washington, D.C.; 14–15, United States suburbs; 20, United States farmland; 21, suburban Washington, D.C.; 22, Los Angeles; 23, New Jersey; 24, London; 25, Los Angeles; 26, 156–65, *Schrebergärten*, Münster, Germany; 27, tomatoes in an Edible Estate; 36, 37, 41, Kansas City, Missouri; 38, rural Minnesota; 39, 42, New Jersey; 40, 43, Los Angeles; 54–55, irrigated farmland in Nevada; 57, London Edible Estate; 58 far right; 60, Cox yard before Edible Estate planted; 61 left, Stan and Priti Cox; 61 right, Kansas prairie; 63 center through 64 left, street views of Cox Edible Estate; 64–68; 70 Foti family and yard before Edible Estate planted; 73 right, street view of Foti Edible Estate; 74–81; 84–86; 89 right, street view of Maplewood; 92 bottom right; 93 bottom left and bottom right; 108; 111 top; 116; 122 bottom two; 122–23 top; 126; 127 right; 128–30; 132 top, bottom left, and bottom right; 133 top and bottom center; 134; 136; 137; 142 right **Curtis Hamilton for the Canary Project,** front flap (right, third down); 58 middle left and middle right; 88, Christman-Wei family and yard before Edible Estate planted; 91; 92 top and bottom left; 93 top and bottom center; 94; 95 *Jones' views of the seats, mansions, castles, etc. of noblemen & gentlemen in England, Wales, Scotland & Ireland...*, vol. 2 of *Jones' Great Britain illustrated*, with plates engraved from drawings by J. P. Neale, London: Jones and Co., 1829–[1831?], inside front cover, Alscot Park, Gloucestershire, England; 17 top, Aynho, Northamptonshire, England; inside back cover, Farming Woods, Northamptonshire, England **Katrina Kennedy,** 148 middle left **Library of Congress,** 2–3, 16–17, Monticello, Charlottesville, Virginia **Los Angeles Public Library,** 4, victory garden; 18, 19, victory gardens, Los Angeles **Sunshine Mathon,** front flap (bottom left), 107 right, 109, 110, 111 bottom three **J Muzacz,** 150 **C. G. Ochsner,** 6, Haeg family on a visit to Los Angeles, 1975 **Beth Olagues,** 148 far left, middle right, and far right **Taidgh O'Neill,** front flap (right, second down), 82–83, 87 **Heiko Prigge,** front flap (bottom right); 96, London garden before Edible Estate planted; 97 right; 99–101; 102 bottom three; 103–5 **Clarence Ridgley,** 125 far right **Jane Sebire,** 102 top **Dorothy Stark,** 153 **Lesley Stern,** Stern house: 44, original yard; 45, yard dug up; 46, working in yard; 47, garden **Leah Swann,** 151 **Stacy Switzer,** 66 **U.S. Geological Survey (http://nationalmap.gov),** 63 left, aerial view of Salina; 73 left, satellite view of Los Angeles; 73 center, aerial view of Lakewood; 89 left, aerial view of Maplewood; 107 left, aerial view of Austin; 115 left, aerial view of Baltimore; 127 left, aerial view of La Cañada Flintridge; 135 left, aerial view of Manhattan **Official White House photo—United States Government work,** 10–11

Project director: Diana Murphy
Design and production: Kimberly Varella, Department of Graphic Sciences (1st edition); Stacy Wakefield (2nd edition)
Separations and printing: Asia Pacific Offset, Inc., China

Set in AauxPro and Alwyn and printed on Cougar opaque smooth, Gold East matte, and KP Fancy Kraft

Library of Congress Cataloging-in-Publication Data

Edible estates : attack on the front lawn / with texts by Will Allen ... [et al.]. -- 2nd ed.
p. cm.
"A project by Fritz Haeg."
Includes bibliographical references.
ISBN 978-1-935202-12-7
1. Edible landscaping. 2. Lawns. 3. Gardening. I. Allen, Will, 1949- II. Haeg, Fritz.
SB475.9.E35E35 2010
712'.6--dc22

2009044639

Metropolis Books is a joint publishing program of:

D.A.P./Distributed Art Publishers, Inc.
155 Sixth Avenue, 2nd floor
New York NY 10013
TEL 212 627 1999 FAX 212 627 9484
www.artbook.com

and

Metropolis Magazine
61 West 23rd Street, 4th floor
New York NY 10010
TEL 212 627 9977 FAX 212 627 9988
www.metropolismag.com

Available through D.A.P./Distributed Art Publishers, Inc., New York

"By attacking the front lawn, an essential icon of the American Dream,
my hope is to ignite a chain reaction of thoughts that question
other antiquated conventions of home, street, neighborhood, city,
and global networks that we take for granted."

Fritz Haeg, preface

"Beauty is a rather more complex concept that has cultural and
moral dimensions. Will you look at this established icon deemed beautiful
for generations with the same eyes once you know the effects it
has on our environment?"

Diana Balmori, "Beauty and the Lawn: A Break with Tradition"

"My Edible Estates . . . are schoolyards and vacant lots, abandoned tracts
of brownfield land, any plot of any size and condition that can be used to
grow food right in the middle of the community that needs it."

Will Allen, "Growing Power: Milwaukee's Urban Farm"

"For if lawn mowing feels like copying the same sentence over and over,
gardening is like writing out new ones, an infinitely variable process of
invention and discovery."

Michael Pollan, "Why Mow? The Case Against Lawns"

"Ripping up the lawn is a beginning, a small gesture of defiance
against the grid. But it is also a way of messing with the border
between the private and the public, of entering that zone
where the domestic encounters the foreign."

Lesley Stern, "The Great Grid"

"I soon discovered that by nature, gardening in the front yard is
a communal experience. I never knew who might stop and share a
garden-inspired story with me when I was in the garden."

Rosalind Creasy, "My House in the Garden"